THE NATURE OF HUMANITY AND THE STATE OF AMERICA

A Unified Theory of the Social World

D0771675

Craig R. Lundahl

University Press of America,® Inc.
Lanham • New York • Oxford

Copyright © 1999
University Press of America,® Inc.
4720 Boston Way
Lanham, Maryland 20706

12 Hid's Copse Rd.
Cumnor Hill, Oxford OX2 9JJ

Library of Congress Cataloging-in-Publication Data

Lundahl, Craig R.
The nature of humanity and the state of America : a unified theory of
the social world / Craig R. Lundahl.
p.   cm.
Includes bibliographical references and index.
1. United States—Moral conditions. 2. United States—Social
conditions—1980- I. Title.
HN90.M6L86   1998   306'.0973—dc21   98-49107 CIP

ISBN 0-7618-1304-7 (cloth: alk. ppr.)
ISBN 0-7618-1305-5 (pbk: alk. ppr.)

⊖™ The paper used in this publication meets the minimum
requirements of American National Standard for Information
Sciences—Permanence of Paper for Printed Library Materials,
ANSI Z39.48—1984

Dedicated To

The Lawgiver

"In every generation there has to be some fool who will speak the truth as he sees it."

Boris Pasternak

Contents

List of Tables and Figures

Foreword

Those who read this book will be either infuriated or enthralled by it. Since it is a book designed to reintroduce God, morality, and spiritual awareness into the study of society.

Dr. Lundahl is a sociologist and is firmly convinced that the discipline of sociology can contribute to an understanding of the human condition. But more importantly, he believes that it is a key to resolving and solving many of the major social ills plaguing mankind.

I have attended many national and regional meetings of sociologists over the years and it is increasingly apparent that the vast majority of those attending these meetings are less interested in furthering sociology as a discipline than they are in using sociology and the meetings as a forum for pursuing personal ideologies and agendas. While not intending to demean the desire of specific groups to improve their personal and collective societal positions, their efforts are not unifying. They are not searching for information or data or methodologies to improve society, but rather to improve the state of others like themselves. They often seem to be more interested in using sociology to further their own reputations than in building sociological theory or in testing research methodologies. Therefore the discipline of sociology has become fragmented into Black Sociology, Hispanic Sociology, Feminist Sociology, Gay Sociology, Christian Sociology, and Islamic Sociology, to name just a few. Subspecialties in sociology have also proliferated to reflect the concerns of various sociologists, i.e. medical, urban, rural, deviance, criminal, children, family, religion, education, and marriage. Even those espousing one of the major historical traditions in sociology, specifically Symbolic Interaction, Conflict, and Structural-Functionalism, often find their attention diverted away from the discipline as a whole.

It is the stated object of this book to attempt to create a unified theory of the social world and this necessitates moving beyond specific agendas and personal interests to examining the "Big Picture." Dr. Lundahl, through the writings of sociologists, social philosophers, psychologists, economists, historians, political scientists, theologians, and legal scholars, presents a coherent theoretical model for the understanding of individuals, society, and the workings of social systems.

In creating his theoretical model he identifies those factors that are critical for any society where individual growth is to be maximized but without trampling the rights of other members of the society. He demonstrates that a shared collective consciousness, i.e. a belief that group interests must exceed individual desires, is necessary for harmonious interaction. To have this collective consciousness, society must rediscover the spiritual quotient, to recognize that man is more than a mere biological machine that is created, functions for a while, and then ends. In other words, man is more than a mass of cells; man has a soul—a spirit that came to the body from a different realm, a divine realm. An increased focus on man's common origin could shift attention to what we all have in common rather than emphasizing our differences.

The spiritual quotient is not new to sociological inquiry, but has increasingly been displaced by the implications of the industrial revolution, urbanization, mass migration, and more recently the information processing revolution. When matters relating to the spiritual quotient have been studied, the focus has tended to be on religious institutions rather than spirituality per se.

Dr. Lundahl's discussion on the need for spirituality to be reintroduced into mainstream sociology will generate considerable controversy as it will most likely be confused with religious dogma and institutional affiliation. However the spiritual dimension rises above specific institutional affiliation. It is the knowledge that all of humanity has a common beginning, that we all have common objectives on earth, and that we all have a common potential destiny. Rather than dividing people into camps feuding with each other over dogma, the focus should be on viewing each other as members of the same family, unique but, at the same time, the same. In a society where truth is relative, where beauty is in the eye of the beholder, where political correctness is more important than scientific rigor, the idea that there are absolute standards for weighing ideas will necessitate major conceptual changes.

Dr. Lundahl's argument that the family is the basic building block of society will also rub many so called social scientists the wrong way. But his arguments are backed by scholarly research, by historical precedent, and by cross-cultural data. By extension, social scientists need to focus more attention on how to preserve the family than on documenting its demise.

In the concluding chapters, Dr. Lundahl uses his theory and it's associated laws to make recommendations as to what must be done to achieve a society whose members will be more concerned about each other than about themselves and where a majority of social ills will be addressed in a positive, constructive, and achievable manner.

Dr. Lundahl is obviously an optimist, but he is not just a dreamer. He has great faith in sociology and in the human spirit and believes that sociologists can make a difference. Many people who read this book might argue that people are so self centered, so materialistic, so caught up in the pursuits of the good life that is is unrealistic to assume that they will change. Dr. Lundahl has identified the source of viable change. It is the family and the recognition of the importance of our spiritual origins, who we are, and our relationship with the rest of the human family.

I would strongly recommend *The Nature of Humanity and the State of America* as serious informative reading for any student who is concerned about the problems plaguing mankind and the deteriorating condition of the family and society.

Harold A. Widdison, Ph.D.
Sociologist
Northern Arizona University

Preface

It has been more than 30 years since an attempt has been made to construct a comprehensive explanation of the social world. Even so, sociology still lacks such a unified theory. Furthermore, since the founding of sociology 160 years ago, it has yet to agree upon or delineate any major social laws even though the Father of Sociology Auguste Comte felt that as a discipline sociology should seek to identify such laws.

Now more than ever before in the history of the world, with all its complexity and overwhelming social problems, there is an urgent need for the knowledge sociology possesses. In earlier years, sociology contributed to solving society's social problems. Then, a problem orientation or an applied approach was the dominant trend in European and American sociology. However, since the 1940s sociology has been primarily a closed debating society with a focus on "pure science" and contributing to knowledge for its own sake with very little inclination to go into society and utilize such knowledge to solve any of the practical problems in society such as crime and poverty. Today, sociology seems to be in quandary over whether to become involved, and if so, just how much. As a result, society has relied upon other disciplines and seldom looked to sociologists for help even though sociology is the discipline that should be most able to help society. It is help that is still desperately needed.

This book proposes a unified theory of the social world for providing a better understanding of social processes in society and the major laws regulating them that could help society solve many if not most of its problems.

However, a real problem today is the refusal to change our scientific explanations considering new information. The historian, Daniel Boorstin, has pointed out that the two major enemies of discovery are the disciples of discoverers and the professions. Disciples turn their discoverer's ideas into dogma and the professions are organized for the maintenance of the traditional approaches to knowledge.

Scientists spend most of their time doing what Thomas S. Kuhn calls "normal science," that is, attempting to establish the truth of the dominant explanation of the scientific community. Scientists tend to see what they have studied and been trained to see in their research. So instead of being neutral scientists as they should be, they become advocates and defenders of the established and dominant explanation. That is why a dominant explanation tends to remain the accepted explanation of the scientific community even if it is not supported by the findings from scientific study. Any change of a dominant explanation in science is revolutionary and a well-established scientific theory or explanation is not changed or abandoned very often.

Any new explanation such as the one found in this book should not be rejected without a hearing just because it may encroach on someone's territory and challenge their existing ideas and theories. There should be a willingness to study and consider any explanation even if it may require a radical change in a dominant explanation. Even if scientists do not agree with or accept every element of a new explanation, they should not discount the whole explanation until there is sufficient evidence to do so.

It is the author's hope that the readers of this volume will keep an open mind as they study this unified explanation of social nature and its related universal laws. The real question should be whether or not the theory describes the reality of the social world.

The purpose of this book is to present an explanation or theory of the social world—a comprehensive description and explanation of the human condition—and the present decline of American Civilization. It is an explanation that attempts to classify and organize events and things in the world. It is an explanation that attempts to explain and predict social phenomena in the world and the United States. Finally, it is an explanation that attempts to make things in the world sensible or understandable. This unified and comprehensive explanation is a foundation for a general understanding of the human condition.

To establish this explanation of the social world, heavy reliance has been placed on several sources of information. The first major source of information for this study is found in the discipline of sociology. Sociology is a social science that has been concerned with the study of human society and social behavior. Even though sociology has been moving away from general theories or explanations that dominated the field over 30 years ago, it has accumulated information that is particularly useful for understanding individual behavior and relationships in society, the institutions of society, and society itself. Two areas of study in sociology that shed particularly important insights into the operation of society have been the study of social stratification and the study of the family. The study of social stratification has received considerable attention by sociologists since World War II while the scientific study of family began about 1920, even though work on the family by the French sociologist Frederic Le Play in the nineteenth century was its forerunner.

Another major source of information is historical information. History discloses that in era after era of time the same or similar difficulties and problems of today have been met. History also discloses that for the most part history is the history of the human mind or ideas; ideas that have shaped the course of humanity. Probably one of the basic limitations of our current analyses of the world is the lack of focus on long-term historical processes. Large-scale historical forces have been at work over centuries to shape humankind's destiny. We tend to pay too little attention to history and the characterization of these long-term trends. Further, humanity simply fails to learn from history for whatever reason. For the most part, we live exclusively in the present, with only some understanding of the recent past. We can learn a great deal about the present as well as the future of the world by just looking at its past. People really need to read and study more history for understanding society today and in the future. The German philosopher Frederick Hegel once made a statement to the effect that those who do not read history will have to repeat it. The Spanish poet and philosopher George Santayana made a similar statement when he said, "Those who cannot remember the past are condemned to repeat it." That is exactly what humanity has done century after century. Today, it seems people are no different from those who preceded them in understanding history. Allan Bloom suggests that in the United States today young people lack an understanding of the past and a vision of the future.

Although this book relies heavily on two major sources of information, that is not to say that other fields will not be used. Generally, sociology and the social sciences today are fragmented into many separate schools and specializations that require drawing on many of them in constructing a comprehensive explanation of humanity. The posing of questions by humanity cannot be answered by any one field and must be sought in several fields even in fields outside science when they provide particularly relevant insights into truth. This search is not restricted by the arbitrary boundaries of knowledge established by the various fields of study.

I hope this book will provide all people, sociologists and students of society as well, with a better understanding of the social world and the present state of the leader of the world community, America, so that through a collective understanding and effort a world of happiness, peace, equality, and prosperity for all its citizens can be achieved.

Acknowledgments

I wish to acknowledge my intellectual debt to the many teachers who were influential in my gaining of knowledge and understanding.

I am also indebted to the theorists who spent their lifetimes in search of an understanding of the social world, those historians who recorded the history of the world from ancient times to recent times, and others who have shared their insights and wisdom about life. Their work served as a springboard in preparing this book. I only hope I have honored their efforts in this work and search for the truth.

I am grateful to all those who have crossed my path in life and shared their lives with me even if it may have been for only a short time. They gave me growth and experience and I owe them much.

My fellow students during my education and my own students at Western New Mexico University were a stimulus to me for which I am grateful.

My love and appreciation for my wife and immediate and extended family, who have been a vitally important support for this work.

I am grateful for the brief moments of inspiration that have assisted me in this endeavor.

I express my appreciation to my friend and colleague Harold A. Widdison who graciously wrote the foreword for this book.

Finally, I thank University Press of America for undertaking this publication project and offering a forum for the presentation of this work. I wish to express my thanks to Nancy J. Ulrich, Acquisitions Editor, and Helen Hudson, Production Editor, and their staff for their advice and assistance with this project.

Chapter 1

Introduction

What can be said about the nature of humanity and America at the closing of the 20th century and the dawning of the 21st century?

The nature of humanity has been pondered by the minds of the world's greatest thinkers. Throughout the recorded history of humanity, humankind has searched to know the world and itself. Humanity has tried to make sense out of what it sees around itself and to grasp what is going on in the world. Today, at major learning centers around the world there is a continuing search underway about humanity's place in the cosmos. Many also ask what is occurring in America as well. The state of America today is the center of considerable discussion among its scholars and others.

Is it possible to answer these questions? Never has there been more information available in the world for doing so. Every day, every field of endeavor is bombarded with facts, data, theories, reports, opinions, and commentaries. This mass of information swirls around in mind-boggling proportions as does the growing technological ability to collect, assemble, organize, and manipulate it. Information technologies today can transmit the entire contents of the 30 volumes of the *Encyclopedia Britannica* in a few seconds. Humanity's knowledge of the world has expanded more in the last century than in all preceding ages combined. In just the last fifteen years, humanity's knowledge has expanded tenfold. Ninety percent of our scientific knowledge has been discovered during the past fifteen years. It is now estimated that by the year 2010 the world's knowledge will have doubled four times. Humanity is no doubt living in the midst of the world's greatest knowledge explosion.

Even with all this information and the technology to collect and organize it, more and more people seem confused and find themselves bewildered about the world and about life. John Naisbitt and Patricia Aburdene wrote in *Megatrends* that, "We are drowning in information and starved for knowledge."1 Similarly, humanity seems to know so much, yet has learned so little about the world and about life.

There seems to be a cry for a sorting, sifting, prioritizing, and integrating of all this information into some sense of wholeness that will give an explanation of humanity. There is a need to provide an understanding of the reality of the world and the people in this world in terms that can be understood by all.

A Single Unified Explanation of Humanity

In the study of the social world, there has never been a complete picture or body of explanatory ideas that everyone accepted as true. Ideally, the work of social scientists is to look for such a single unified explanation or model of the world—variously called a unified theory, a general theory, a complete theory, or a comprehensive theory—to explain all social phenomena. When we do discover such a theory or explanation, it should in time be understandable by everyone. It should be an explanation that makes sense of something that is otherwise not understood. It should contain the basic principles of truth. It should also account for reality—for the ultimate test of such an explanation will be whether it explains reality accurately.

Is there such an explanation today? No, there is no such explanation today that is accepted as true. Will there be such a theory or explanation in the future? Yes. In fact, the knowledge for such an explanation has been acquired by humanity. Its sources are knowledge documented in individual observations and the findings of historical and scientific studies. Most of this knowledge is not necessarily new but more appropriately should be described as rediscovered. It has been said that there is nothing new under the sun, that old ideas tend to reappear which are never clothed in exactly the same fashion. In other words, the past is now and the future has already happened. Perhaps what is new about the explanation in this book is the organization in the presentation of this knowledge accumulated over the ages into a new elementary unified explanation of the social world that is partially supported by scientific investigation.

Many people in the world think theories or explanations are not at all useful, but this is not true. For the social philosopher Socrates (469-399 BC), the central philosophical issue was the very practical theoretical question of how should one live. Flight would be impossible without theoretical ideas regarding the physical universe. The treatment of diseases is based on theoretical ideas on the cause and operation of diseases. The stock market rests on some basic theoretical understandings. Even the course of history is affected by theorical ideas as demonstrated dramatically by the work of Karl Marx. Thus, theories are useful for not only flight, the treatment of diseases, and the stock market, but also for the living of people's lives and understanding societies and the world people live in. Unified explanations of the world influence how people see it, understand it, explain it, act in it, and thus, what it will become.

The Purpose of the Book

The purpose of this book is to describe the decline of American Civilization and to explain how this has occurred by presenting a new, sensible, and comprehensive description and explanation that explains the human condition. This unified and comprehensive explanation is a foundation for a general understanding of the human condition in the world and America.

The main objective of this book is to describe the general nature of humanity with a secondary objective of describing the state of American society. This effort will include describing and examining the decline of America, the basic principles or laws that operate in the world, the major determinant of social behavior, the consequences of social behavior, the general patterns or operation of society, the forces in the world and their affect on humanity, the good society, and how to restore America to her former greatness.

Organization of the Book

In this book, a comprehensive explanation and understanding of the social world and the decline of America is described in 12 chapters. Following this introduction, is Chapter 2. In this chapter, a very brief survey of the explanation of the world is given. This survey includes an outline of the basic assumptions for explaining the nature of humanity. The rest of the book presents different aspects of the explanation that are needed for a better understanding of the overall explanation and an application of it to the state of American society. Chapter 3 describes and demonstrates the current state and well-being of America. Four destructive trends contributing to America's decline are also described in Chapter 3. The remainder of the book provides an understanding of how the United States got to its current state. In Chapter 4, the social laws that govern the social world are outlined and briefly discussed. A key factor ignored by science, yet so vitally important in affecting humankind and society, is the spiritual factor. This factor is examined in Chapter 5. In Chapter 6, the basic element of society, the individual, is analyzed. The composition of the individual, the origins of the personality, the process of human thought, human growth and development, and the character of the individual is described in this analysis of the individual. The connecting links between individuals and their societies—social relationships—is described in Chapter 7. Next, the keystone of society, the family, is described in Chapter 8. In this chapter, the importance of the institution of family is emphasized and its relationship to other institutions is briefly described as well as its change and most important function. The topic of Chapter 9 is society. The types of societies and their characteristics, the social order of these societies and how they develop and change, their cycle, and the greatest threat to a society is explained in this chapter. The good society and its economy is described in Chapter 10. In Chapter 11, the keys for the restoration of America are outlined. In the final chapter, Chapter 12, are some final thoughts on the well-being of the world, its great potential and the strong possibility of its collapse, and the keys for capitalizing on the world's potential for eliminating decay, suffering, and unhappiness.

Chapter 2

Overview

A good theory or explanation tells a general story of the workings of humanity and should closely parallel the actual operation of human life. Two major attempts to produce such a general explanation of social life are called "functional theory" and "conflict theory." According to functional theory, societies are made up of several parts such as families, businesses, and churches who cooperate with each other in contributing to the continued operation and stability of society. Social life is governed by consensus and cooperation. The other explanation of social life–conflict theory–sees societies experiencing conflict among competing interest groups and instability with the likelihood of rapid change. According to this theory some members of society dominate other members through coercion and even force and social life involves conflict because of differing goals. Neither of these explanations have stood the test of time or research even though parts of them may be true. The research done by social scientists has failed to support completely functional theory or conflict theory as providing a comprehensive explanation of social life. Consequently, a completely accurate general explanation of social life is still a future goal. (For a comparison of functional and conflict theories as well as symbolic interactionism and evolutionary theory to the theory offered in this book see the Appendix.)

The explanation in this book is an attempt to provide only the beginning of such a comprehensive explanation of how the social world really works, and in turn, an explanation of the state of

America at the end of the Twentieth Century. All explanations of the social world are based on a set of assumptions that are assumed to be true but may not yet be proven true. In this chapter, an overview of a new explanation is presented to you by describing its elementary assumptions. Please keep in mind that this explanation is an attempt to describe some very general patterns that operate across time in the social world. After describing the state of American society, the next six chapters of the book presents more detailed information needed for a more complete understanding and knowledge of this explanation.

According to this explanation, universal principles or social laws govern the social world. With few exceptions, the first 100 years of the scientific discipline of sociology can be characterized as a search by various sociologists for the basic laws of the social universe. It was the founder and father of sociology, the French social philosopher Auguste Comte (1798-1857), who advocated a science of society in the early decades of the 19th century. He visualized sociology as a discipline that would seek to discover the laws of human organization.1 Even though there is almost a total absence of proven sociological laws, such laws have always operated in the social universe and some have been known by humanity from time to time. It is under these laws that the social world operates.

The basic element of any society is the individual. The individual is a personality consisting of a spirit and a body and is made up of all of life's experiences. Each individual passes through a number of distinct transitions or phases, that are often social and biological in nature simultaneously. As individuals pass through these phases of life they meet with various life events or problems requiring them to use their agency to select various courses of action. These life events or problems give them experience and human growth. Every choice made by an individual leads to the development of the individual's character. The character of the individual is his or her innermost motivations and thoughts based on values that lead to actions and behavior. Each individual chooses the kind of life they will live and what he or she will be. In essence, life is the sum of the individual's thoughts.

The social structure of every society is made up of the patterned social relationships among individuals and groups. These social relationships occur in the context of a variety of socially defined positions that people occupy in society. The essence of this web of social interaction lies in the rights and obligations that people in different positions have to one another as defined by the normative system of society. This system tells people how to behave in particular social situations. It is individuals and groups interacting with each other that accomplish the activities of society and constitute the actions of society.

The actions of every member of society, no matter how small their sphere of influence, are very important because all actions have individual and societal consequences. Obviously, some actions are more important than others. It is the actions of individuals in compliance or noncompliance particularly with the *Law of Spirituality* that results in different individual as well as societal consequences. If this law is followed, compliance with the other laws will follow since all laws hang on the *Law of Spirituality*.

In essence then, society becomes the sum of what its members do in their lives. It is society's members who create society's social life. Those societies whose individuals collectively live the *Law of Shared Resources* generally experience happiness, peace, morality, equality, and prosperity.

A society or a world can never be changed unless its citizens change first. Once the members of society start embracing materialistic values, the society begins to move toward social and spiritual decline. As the members of society pursue materialistic values they begin to work for wealth, power, and status, and to accumulate wealth. Wealth now becomes the measure of success in society. This results in the members of society dividing into classes with each competing for wealth, power, and status. This desire for wealth, power, and status leads to inequality and immorality.

Any society whose members collectively fail to live the *Law of Shared Resources* generally experience unhappiness, conflict, immorality, inequality, and suffering.

Eventually, materialism and inequality can destroy society. This can only be avoided by a change in the values and the actions of members in society, and an economic system that is in tune with the universal laws, particularly the *Law of Spirituality* and the *Law of Shared Resources*.

These elementary assumptions can be stated as follows:

1. Universal social principles or laws govern the social world.
2. Individuals using their agency choose various courses of action.
3. Every human action and activity in compliance or noncompliance, particularly with the *Law of Spirituality,* results in different individual and societal consequences.

4. It is individuals socially interacting with each other that constitute the actions of society.
5. A society is the sum of what its members do in their lives.
6. A society living the *Law of Shared Resources* generally experiences happiness, peace, morality, equality, and prosperity.
7. A society begins to break the *Law of Shared Resources* when its members start pursuing materialistic values.
8. A society that fails to live the *Law of Shared Resources* generally experiences unhappiness, conflict, immorality, inequality, and suffering.
9. Societies who continue to break the *Law of Shared Resources* will eventually fail.
10. A society can return to conformity with the *Law of Shared Resources* as its members begin to pursue spiritual values.

This completes the overview. The remainder of the book will describe the state of American society and why America finds itself in this state and elaborate in more detail on a proposed explanation on the nature of humanity.

Chapter 3

The State of America

Is America in decline? The term decline is often used to refer to moral decline, which in essence is a loss of spirituality. The decline of any society or civilization is always preceded by a loss of spirituality and an increase in materialism (the *Law of Social Change)*, just as an increase in spirituality precedes the rise of a society or civilization. This change, from a spiritual to a material value system eventually leads to division, inequality, and immorality in society, and therefore, moral decline.

Regarding the question of decline in America, some professional observers of American society would say there is no decline in America. They would probably suggest that America is simply undergoing change as a result of new information technology, something that is characteristic of an information society or postmodern society. Unfortunately, these observers as do many citizens suffer from what might be called the "All is Well Syndrome." The All is Well Syndrome means the rationalization of a profound social crisis to the point of its acceptance as okay or the denial of a profound social crisis into nonexistence. What happens is people adjust to the social crisis and accept it as reality. Very similar to this Syndrome is what United States Senator Daniel Patrick Moynihan has described as "normalizing."1 It is an effort by a society experiencing very high levels of deviant behavior to accommodate the behavior by normalizing it. The gradual normalization of aberration was also recognized earlier by the English poet Alexander Pope

(1688-1744) when he wrote that when vice begins to occur often and becomes too familiar, people will at first endure it, then pity it, and eventually embrace it.2

Not only do people accept their deteriorating situation as normal but they begin to lose their sense of good and evil, and actually, begin to call evil good and good evil. This pattern has been observed through history as societies and civilizations neared collapse. It seems the closer they approached collapse the more difficult it was for them to recognize the danger they faced and to recognize their eminent demise. This is a universal characteristic of collapsing societies.

Some historians, sociologists, theologians, and others including many citizens have recognized and declared the decline occurring in America but their warnings have generally gone unheeded. Today, indexes showing the cultural decline of America are being published annually. One such index is the Index of Social Health prepared by Marc L. Miringoff and published by the Fordham University Institute for Innovation in Social Policy.3 This index shows the incidence of 17 social problems such as children in poverty, teen suicide, drug abuse, homicide, and the gap between the rich and poor. Another index prepared by former Education Secretary William Bennett and published by Empower America is the Index of Leading Cultural Indicators. It is composed of 19 social indicators such as divorce, drug use, and teen births.4 Both these indexes report that America's social problems are getting progressively worse.

However, these indexes tend to examine the symptoms of the root cause or determinant of the decline in America but not the real cause. The leading cause of decline in any society is the loss of spirituality and the values it engenders. As will be pointed out later, all universal laws hang on the *Law of Spirituality* or the level of spirituality. Therefore, if there is a loss of spirituality at the individual level it is translated into a loss at the society level (the *Law of Collective Spirituality*). This in turn will affect the collective values of society (the *Law of Collective Values*) that determine the strivings and actions (the *Law of Collective Action*) of society's members and changes in the society's social structure (the *Law of Social Change*). The loss of spirituality always moves society toward the condition of materialism and the values it engenders as well as the loss of charity, family destruction, the division of society into classes, the unequal distribution of wealth, the breakdown of social relationships, and immoral behavior.

If the well-being of any society is to be evaluated, then certain actions or behaviors of its citizens must be examined. To understand the character of a person, study what he or she says and does, or in other words, study their actions or behavior. The same holds true for societies. If you want to understand a society's character examine its collective actions or behavior.

Societal Well-Being

The most important human behaviors for evaluating the state of a society are charitable behaviors, marriage and family behaviors, economic, materialistic, and stratifying behaviors, deviant behaviors, social interactive behaviors, and social behaviors. On the following two pages is a table labeled "Index of Societal Well-Being." This Index includes these important human behaviors for the functioning of society, their social measures, the more important of many social indicators of these behaviors for determining the state of America's well-being, and some measurements. Although it is in a rudimentary stage of development and requires further refinement, it does serve the purpose of providing an approximation of America's well-being.

The Index begins with the social measure of charity for examining charitable behavior. The social indicator to measure charity is contributions to charitable organizations by the rich. Although the index does not examine the contributions to charitable organizations by the poor, the poor may actually be more generous and compassionate than the rich. A Gallup Poll in 1988 found that households with income below $10,000 gave 2.8 percent of their earnings, while those with incomes between $50,000 and $75,000 gave only 1.5 percent.5 Furthermore, the more wealthy people usually give after their primary goal of the good life is achieved, and even then, their charity is often the result of some ulterior motive such as the need to save taxes. In the book, *Charity Begins At Home,* Teresa Odendahl's study of rich charity shows that over two-thirds of their charitable giving goes to elite non-profit institutions like elite universities and prep schools, museums, private hospitals, and the like so that their tax deductible donations end up funding their own interests.6 This certainly raises questions of the usefulness of this measure even though it is presented. A related measure not utilized here is volunteerism that consists of only about 8 million volunteers working in "human services," a broad category that includes aiding the homeless and family counseling, and approximately 85 million doing what Pastor Eugene F. Rivers III calls "recreational

Table 3.1   Index of Societal Well-Being

Social Activity	Type of Behavior	Social Measure	Social Indicator	Measurements	Rank and Societal Well-Being Index Scores
Charity	Charitable Behavior	Charity	Contributions	Millionaires gave 7% of income after taxes to charity in 1979 and 4% in 1990	7
Family	Marriage and Family Behavior	Family Structure	Two-Parent Family Type	87.1% two-parent families in 1970 and 71.9% two-parent families in 1990	6
		Family Destruction	Abortion	2.8 abortions per 100 women in 1985	5
			Divorce	44% to 66% of marriages will divorce today	
			Employed Mothers (Preschool Children)	19% in 1960 and 59% in 1990	
			Fatherless Families	11.5% in 1970 and 24.2 % in 1990	
			Infidelity	50% of husbands and 30 to 40% of wives	
			Unwed Mothers	Illegitimacy per 100 births was 5 in 1960 and 30 in 1991	
Inequality	Economic, Materialistic, and Stratifying Behavior	Wealth	Distribution of Wealth	Top 5th of population possessed 78.7% of wealth in 1983 and 80% in 1990 and bottom 5th -.4% and -1% in 1983 and 1990	3
			Distribution of Income (Gini Index of Income Inequality)	Top 5th received 42.7% of income in 1983 and 44.2% in 1991 and bottom 5th 4.7% in 1983 and 4.5% in 1991; Gini Index in 1967 was .348 and in 1991 it was .397	
			Poverty Rate	Poverty rate was 12.1% in 1969 and 15.1% in 1993 (40% for those under 18 years old)	
		Power	Political Power Concentration	367 corporations with assets exceeding $1 billion, represent 71% of all corporate assets and 73% of total corporate profit	3
		Prestige	Occupational Prestige	Occupational prestige high and low scores from 1972-93 of physician of 86 and shoe shiner of 9 for a score difference of 77	2

Table 3.1   Index of Societal Well-Being (Continued)

Social Activity	Type of Behavior	Social Measure	Social Indicator	Measurements	Rank and Societal Well-Being Index Scores
Inequality	Economic, Materialistic, and Stratifying Behavior	Class Structure	Classes	No classes in 1890 case (Middletown) and six classes consisting of the Capitalist Class, Upper Middle Class, Middle Class, Working Class, Working Poor, and the Underclass in 1990	1
Immorality	Deviant Behavior	Crime	Crime Index	The Crime Index in 1965 was 2,000 crimes per 100,000 population to 5,660 crimes in 1992	4
			Crime Rates	Violent Crime Rate of 150 crimes per 100,000 population in 1960 to 750 in 1990 Property Crime Rate of 1,880 crimes per 100,000 population in 1960 to 5,100 in 1990	
Social Relation-ships	Social Interactive Behavior	Social Relations	Hate Crimes	7,600 incidents in 1993 and increasing	6
			Legal Conflicts	Three times as many lawsuits in 1990 than in 1960	
Social Values	Social Behavior	Social Values	Trust in Institutions	Confidence in institutions in 1966 and in 1989—military, 61% and 32%; colleges, 61% and 32%; medicine, 73% and 30%; Supreme Court, 54% and 28%; the press, 30% and 18%; Executive Branch, 41% and 17%; organized religion, 42% and 16%; Congress, 42% and 16%; major companies, 55% and 16%; and labor unions, 22% and 10%	2
			Societal Well-Being Index Score		39

volunteerism."7

The two social measures of family structure and family destruction are used for examining marriage and family behavior in the Index. The social indicator to measure family structure is the two-parent family type that is critical to stable and healthy societies and the major social indicators to measure family destruction are abortion, divorce, employed mothers of preschool children, fatherless families, infidelity, and unwed mothers.

The Index has four social measures for examining economic, materialistic, and stratifying behavior. They are wealth, power, prestige, and class structure. The first three of these measures were described by German sociologist Max Weber (1864-1920) as causes of stratification.8 The social indicators of wealth are the distribution of wealth, the distribution of income and the Gini Index of income inequality (the lower the ratio, the less income inequality; America has more income inequality than most European countries), and the rate of poverty. The concentration of power is the social indicator of power, and occupational prestige is the social indicator of prestige. The social indicator for class structure is the number of classes.

Deviant behavior is the third type of behavior included in the Index. The major measure for examining deviant behavior is crime. The Crime Index and crime rates are the social indicators used for measuring deviant behavior in society.

The Index consists of the social measure of social relations for examining social interactive behavior. The social indicators for measuring social relations are hate crimes and legal conflicts or lawsuits.

A final type of behavior included in the Index is social behavior. The social values of society is the social measure used for examining social behavior. The major social indicator for measuring social values is the confidence citizens have in their social institutions because it is social institutions that embody the social values of society.

The Index is compiled by adding 10 measures (or social variables) of societal well-being related to charity, family, inequality, immorality, social relationships, and social values: (1) charity, (2) family structure, (3) family destruction, (4) wealth, (5) power, (6) prestige, (7) class structure, (8) crime, (9) social relations, and (10) social values. Most of the data for the Index are from official government sources.

Each of the 10 measures of well-being is ranked from 0 to

10—with the most troubling and materialistic being ranked 0. Each measure is assigned 10 points and those points are divided by the number of social indicators for each measure. Then points are assigned equally to the number of measurements for each social indicator.

The 10 measures are added together to obtain the Societal Well-Being Index. Societies displaying giving and sharing, a preponderance of traditional two-parent families, little if any difference in resources between its citizens, little crime, strong and cooperative social relationships, and strong support and confidence in its institutions will score high on the Index.

America's Societal Well-Being Index score is 39. As shown on the Index, in almost every measurement a figure is given for an earlier period of time and a later period of time, which is most often in the 1960s or 1970s and the early 1990s, for comparative purposes. The Index also shows that every measurement is getting progressively worse. The meaning of the score 39 is best understood by rating the Societal Well-Being Index by the following quadrants: High Well-Being, Moderate Well-Being, Poor Well-Being, and Minimal Well-Being. This can be figuratively represented as shown in the figure entitled "Societal Well-Being Index Quadrants and Associated Society Type" on the following page.

The figure shows where America is located among the quadrants, which is at poor societal well-being or Poor Well-Being. This is a very precarious situation for two reasons. First, it is a rating that identifies America as a stalemated society. A "stalemated society" is one that is unable to solve its problems and one that is losing its legitimacy among its citizens, which can eventually lead to the failure of society. There is certainly evidence of both these patterns occurring in America. America is suffering from a pessimism about its institutions and about politicians and the entire governmental process after years of broken promises, legislative gridlock, catering to special interests, and negative political campaigns.

Second, the measurements indicate not only America's precarious situation but also that it is getting progressively worse. America is only approximately 14 points away from a "dysfunctional society;" an unjust society that is overwhelmed by its problems and has lost its legitimacy. Simply put it is a society that does not work anymore and will fail soon—just the opposite of a functional society.

According to the sociologist Daniel E. Rossides, a "functional society" is a problem-solving entity where the citizens can feed

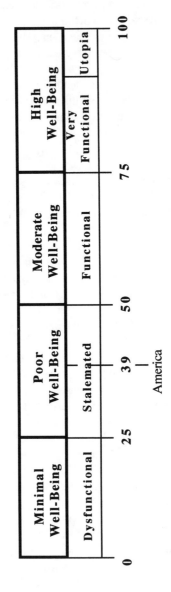

Figure 3.1   Societal Well-Being Index Quadrants and Associated Society Type

themselves, reproduce, settle disputes, and adjust to new conditions. It also has legitimacy because people feel that the power groups in the society deserve their power. The ordinary citizen accepts the hierarchy, laws, taxes, unequal wealth and income, competition, and so on because they see direct and beneficial consequences coming from them. A functional society has positions and rules that tend to produce intended and desired results.9

A "very functional society" operates at an even more efficient level than a functional society because it is a society that is beginning to approximate a spiritual society. It is a society that fosters value orientations guiding beliefs in and behaviors of a higher power and the spirit, humanitarian motives and charity, family traditions and family life, integrity and honesty in social relationships, moral orientation and moral behavior, and equality.

The "utopia" society is the society described in Chapter 10. It is a problem-free society.

Four Destructive Trends in American Society

Today a vast social disaster is unfolding. There are several destructive trends contributing to this unfolding disaster and the undermining of the strength of American society. Four of the more important of these trends are family diversity, the movement toward a two-tiered society and unequal economy, the neglect of society's children, and the development of a new morality.

The Great American Family Experiment

America has embarked on a vast natural experiment in family life. It began in the 1960s and is continuing today. It appears America wants to test whether the family really is the basis of society. It does not seem to matter that history is filled with the debris of civilizations and societies who conducted the same experiment. Unfortunately, America will get the same result.

Unlike the more recent Russian Communist's planned destruction of the family mentioned in chapter 8, the American family experiment has no formal research plan but is the result of breaking universal social principles. Although unintentional, it examines the relationship between family diversity and the undermining of society. However, do not be fooled into believing that family diversity is something healthy and positive and that society is just witnessing a process of evolution. As the two sociologists Brigitte and Peter Berger have noted, family diversity has been quietly translated into a norm of diversity and a new and acceptable morality.10 The results of the American experiment may not yet be quite as spectacular as the Russian experiment but they are very similar. However, the Russians were smart enough to stop their experiment short of disaster.

America has seen the undermining of family authority, the continued movement toward equality of men and women, moral laxness that permits unrestricted sexual relations, laws permitting marriage and divorce at will, legalized abortion, and a smorgasbord of family forms including the fastest growing form, the single-parent family. These developments indicate the breaking up of the American family and the incipient decline and impending death of America.

How did this happen? The sociologist David Popenoe gives some insight into this question. He attributes the movement away from the traditional American family to four major social trends that emerged in the 1960s. These trends signaled a widespread flight from the traditional nuclear family—a family form emphasizing the male as a "good provider," the female as a "good wife and mother," and the paramount importance of the family for childbearing. The major trends were rapid fertility decline, the sexual revolution, the movement of mothers into the labor force, which has led to a destructive revolution in child rearing, and the upsurge in divorce.11

According to Popenoe these trends signaled a widespread retreat from the traditional nuclear family in its dimensions of a lifelong, sexually exclusive unit, focused on children, with a division of labor between husband and wife. He points out that unlike most previous change that reduced family functions and diminished the importance of the kin group, the change of the past 30 years has tended to break up the nucleus of the family unit—the bond between husband and wife. He further notes that during the past 30 years, family decline in the United States has been both steeper and more alarming than during any other quarter-century in the history of America. Of today's American families, no more than 15 percent fit the traditional model and it seems to continue to be declining. If society is to be preserved and to experience well-being, the "traditional family" in its most fundamental form must be preserved.

The Achilles Heel of Advanced Capitalism, Inequality, and the Loss of the American Dream

The prosperity of an advanced capitalist society heavily depends on increasingly higher levels of demand for products. In other words, many people must be willing to part with their earnings if they are going to buy what is being produced. Thus, a "culture of materialism" based on owning and consuming goods and services, is essential to the later stages of industrial capitalism. But what happens when the majority of consumers stop consuming for lack of money. That is exactly what will happen more and more often as America moves toward a "bipolar" or dual society with its even greater inequality and reductions in consumption.

Traditionally, America has had a large middle class. However, the proportion of the middle class population classified by income began to shrink between 1969 and 1986 from 71.2 percent to 63.3 percent, while the number of high- and low-earning families were increasing. Rich families and poor families are continuing to replace middle-class families, a process that is often referred to as "the loss of the American Dream." In fact, there is an increasing concentration of income and wealth among the wealthiest families in America. For example, in 1989, the top 1 percent of American families owned 48 percent of the country's total financial wealth. This is further demonstrated by the ownership of wealth by the top 10 percent of the population in 1774 of 45 percent compared to 55 percent by the other 90 percent of the population, and in 1983, when it was 69 percent and 31 percent respectively.

The trend toward a bipolar America is depicted in the figure on the following page entitled, "The Trend Toward a Bipolar Distribution of American Household Income, 1960s to the 1980s." It shows how the distribution of household income is shrinking the middle class and increasing the size of rich families and poor families, more particularly of poor families and families in poverty.

These changes can be attributed to the growth of industries that tend to employ primarily two tiers of workers—highly trained people who are paid well and unskilled workers who are paid poorly, tax programs favoring wealthy families, corporate downsizing for the sake of greater profits, part-time work, automation, wage instability, and the lower wages of the increasing number of female-headed households. This trend will continue to lead to growing inequality and polarization in all aspects of society. As a result, there is great

Figure 3.2   **The Trend Toward a Bipolar Distribution of American Household Income, 1960s to the 1980s**

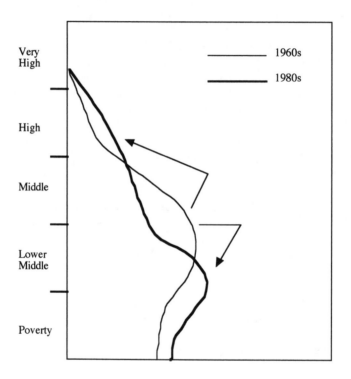

potential for serious social and political conflict, and social disruption is likely as the underclass seek to improve their situation.

This trend is leading to a situation similar to those of Latin American countries with their small middle-class populations and authoritarian governments that invest heavily in police forces to control the poor classes. In these countries, the rich live in walled compounds surrounded by barbed wire, guard dogs, and armed guards to protect themselves. The poor struggle to feed their children and grow angry at a society that offers little hope for improvement. These conditions, obviously, are not conducive to an open democratic society. America already has 20,000 gated communities.

The sociologist Denny Braun put it this way: "To follow a path of economic gluttony, while those around us literally starve, all but guarantees some form of French Revolution for contemporary society."12

The author Barbara Ehrenreich concludes an article on the growing income inequality in America with this statement:

> Everyone has a stake in creating a less anxious, more egalitarian society.... The greatest danger is not that a class-conscious, left-leaning political alternative will arise, but that it will not. For without a potent political alternative, we are likely to continue our slide toward a society divided between the hungry and the overfed, the hopeless and the have-it-alls. What is worse, there will be no mainstream, peaceable political outlets for the frustration of the declining middle class or the desperation of those at the bottom. Instead, it is safe to predict that there will be more crime, more exotic forms of political and religious sectarianism, and ultimately, that we will no longer be one nation, but two.13

The development of a bipolar society also creates extreme inequality that may generate economic disaster. Each of the five major depressions (recessions) in the history of America in the 1780s, 1840s, 1930s, 1970s, and 1980s was preceded by huge and increasing inequalities in wealth and income. Essentially what happens is the poor and middle classes borrow more money to maintain their standard of living until they can borrow no more and their pockets run dry. At that point, they can not buy anymore. They must borrow because they are never paid the same for their services as they pay for the products they helped to produce. In the meantime, the rich have the money and can not possibly consume or buy enough to keep the economy going, so deflation starts, depression results, and the economy comes to a standstill. The capitalist economy of America is depicted in the simplified representation entitled the "The Cycle of Advanced Capitalism" on the following page.

The figure shows only two classes for description purposes, even though it is fairly realistic. The rich or the "haves," is the top ten percent in wealth, and the poor or the "have nots," is everyone else. In an advanced capitalist system, the poor transfer billions in net purchases of goods and services to the rich who essentially produce the goods and services and then the rich pay a "token" tax on the income and make loans with the rest to the government. Then, the government gives almost double that amount in net subsidies or entitlements to the poor. In order to return billions to the lower classes so their purchasing power remains somewhat intact, the government undertaxes the rich, overtaxes the lower classes who bear the heaviest tax burden, and borrows the rest from the upper class and foreign investors, and these creditors (the rich), in turn, shape government policies in their favor. This creates a deficit that always equals the money the rich and foreign investors keep after taxes.

It is the profit motive that keeps this economic system afloat because unless there is a profitable market to exploit the rich who have the resources and who are money or profit oriented will not generally have the incentive to continue to employ people to produce goods and services. The rich cannot profit from trading among themselves because non-equity financial wealth is a zero-sum game. In other words, the rich can wheel and deal with each other all they want but they still end up with the same amount among themselves whether that be a million dollars or a billion dollars or whatever the figure. The amount will not increase unless another group loses money to the rich. That is why capitalism is a bankrupt economic system because somebody has to lose eventually. The course of capitalism has always had a tendency to tendency to make a few rich and to sink the masses of other people into poverty and degradation. For instance, despite a booming economy in America during the current decade, 35 million people still go hungry.

It is also a bankrupt system because of overconsumption. It is a system that encourages overconsumption of resources resulting in deficit spending or buying on credit. There is always a financial deficit resulting from the government borrowing from the rich and other investors to give to the poor through subsidies or entitlements so they can keep buying more and more and losing more and more of their money to the rich. Market capitalism requires citizens to be

Figure 3.3   The Cycle of Advanced Capitalism

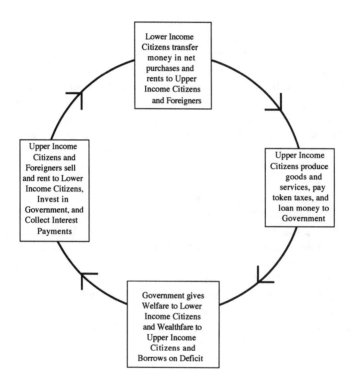

consumers first, to buy now, go into debt, pay later, and enjoy life. In such an economic system, a balanced budget is unlikely because the rich would not be able to make any money unless America runs a trade surplus, which is highly unlikely for America in the current world market unless it can cut consumption. Sooner or later, the economy has to grind to a halt because the poor only have a finite amount of money to spend.

A careful balancing act must be performed by the government if an advanced capitalist economy is to function. The government must return money from taxation and loans to the lower classes so they do not go completely broke and stop buying goods and services and paying rents. If the government cuts too much aid to the poor, there is no demand for goods and services. If the government lowers taxes on the rich too much, it serves no purpose because there is a limit to how much such a small group can buy. Furthermore, the lower taxes will not serve any productive purpose unless there is a profitable market for the rich to exploit.14

Because of our enormous material consumption, America has been running a large internal budget deficit and a large trade deficit since 1977. In addition, (1) huge interest payments to rich and foreign investors, (2) wealthfare to the rich (including corporations) through favorable tax laws, (3) entitlements, (4) large outlays to finance the military (resources used toward rearmament and away from enhancing productivity), (5) federal subsidies to state and local governments, (6) the federal payroll, (7) American capital sent overseas (billions in foreign aid), and (8) the costs of corruption and crime (particularly upper-class or white collar crime) is bringing the economy dangerously close to collapse. Consumption patterns and these expenditures have outstripped the economy's ability to sustain them. It is foreign lenders who are keeping America in business. America is the world's largest debtor.

America must make painful decisions in the next few years if it is to arrest the continuing absolute decline in its standard of living that grows more noticeable with each passing year. Mass consumption must be curbed and inequality must decline to begin to cure our economic (and societal) problems. This inequality is evidenced by wage inequality that has returned to the level found at the end of the 1930s Depression. Differences in income of 60 percent between White and Black Americans, the substantial increase in the ratio between the highest paid manager or CEO and the lowest paid employees in Fortune 500 firms of 29 to 1 in 1979 to over 203 to 1 in 1995, the rich-poor gap of over $50,000, and differences between people who are earning nothing a year to athletes, entertainers, physicians, and business executives who earn millions in a year to recording artists who receive $60 to $80 million dollars for recording a few albums of songs are just a few examples of America's great disparity in income. If the current income trends continue, it has been estimated that by sometime early in the next century the top 4 percent of individuals and families drawing paychecks will earn as much on the job as 60 percent of the rest of American workers. The country must also collect enough tax revenue from the corporations and the rich, reinvest money in productive employment, plant machinery, and research and civilian research and development, and job training, and stop spending huge sums on the military establishment.

It was the French social philosopher Alexis de Tocqueville (1805-1859) who studied American values in the past century that argued in democratic societies, particularly in America, people are preoccupied with increasing their wealth. He said this creates minds preoccupied with the search for practical solutions:

> To minds thus predisposed, every new method which leads by a shorter road to wealth, every machine which spares labor, every instrument which diminishes the cost of production, every discovery which facilitates pleasures or augments them, seems to be the grandest effort of the human intellect.15

He also said that this predisposition leads to a neglect of consideration of primary causes and principles.16

More recently, the economist and historian, Robert L. Heilbroner wrote that:

> No other civilization has permitted the calculus of self-interest so to dominate its culture. It has transmogrified greed and philistinism [or materialism] into social virtues, and subordinated all values to commercial values.17

Pollsters have found more Americans now place a premium on material things than ever, and that they focus much more on money than they did a generation ago. For example, Roper Starch Worldwide polls found that Americans who said they want to earn a lot of money grew from 38 percent in 1975 to 63 percent in 1994. In the annual survey of college freshmen conducted by the Higher Education

Research Institute at UCLA, freshmen who said that it was essential or very important to be very well off financially rose from 41 percent in 1968 to 74 percent in 1995.18

Sociologists are, of course, concerned about the possible social, political, and economic consequences of the trend toward an increasingly bipolar and unequal America. The key to maintaining any economy including capitalism is the equitable distribution of resources. Besides the distribution of resources, it further requires a system that must be based on a new ethic not the corrupt work ethic found today or on the "maximization of profits" found in the business world (this system is described in Chapter 10).

A Fatherless Society and A Lost Generation

The greatest negative consequence of family decline is on the children of this generation. Mainly because of selfishness, family diversity, and fatherlessness, the quality of life for children in the past 30 years has worsened. The general disinvestment in family life because adults are investing in self-fulfillment and less willing to invest time, money, and energy in family life has also resulted in a disinvestment in children's welfare. It is the individual, not the family unit, in whom the main investments increasingly are made. This disinvestment in family life began with men avoiding their parental obligations and responsibilities and with many women forsaking their roles as full-time homemakers. These delinquent adults are producing delinquent children.

America has already lost a substantial portion of the generation of young people under the age of 19, and in so doing, jeopardized its future. They have been lost to alcohol abuse, child abuse and neglect, crime, drug abuse, disease, illiteracy, malnutrition, poor self-esteem, poverty, sexual promiscuity, teen pregnancy, and violence. According to a study by the American Medical Association and the National Association of State Boards of Education there has never been such a generation of young Americans that has been less healthy, less cared for, and less prepared for life than their parents at the same age.19 They are at tremendous risk of failing to lead productive adult lives. America has ignored the fact that children are a long-term investment in the well-being of the nation in the future.

The political scientist Charles Murray points out that the trendlines of Black Americans—of illegitimacy, dropout from the labor force, and crime—all moved rapidly upward when the black illegitimacy rate passed 25 percent, a rate that now stands at approximately 70 percent of births. The same may be expected of White Americans who are fast approaching the 25 percent rate if they have not passed it as births to single white women continue to increase. Murray feels that illegitimacy is the single most important social problem of today because it drives so many other social problems such as crime, drugs, poverty, welfare, illiteracy, and homelessness. He says, if people do not do something about illegitimacy, America will become an authoritarian, socially segregated, centralized state.20

America is now a nation that is dangerously split according to the condition of its youngest citizens—those who come from two-parent families and those from single-parent families, 97 percent of which are fatherless. The former group of children will most likely prosper and the later group will most likely be born into poverty and tend to stay in poverty. Today, 2 out of every 5 children under 18 years of age lives in poverty. Unless current trends are reversed, it is estimated that early in the next century 1 out of every 2 American children will be born out of wedlock and into poverty, the result of the most plaguing sin of this generation—sexual immorality. The sociologist Amitai Etzioni said of the considerable research on single parenting that the body of data leads to the inescapable conclusion that single parenting is harmful to children.21 What may be of more concern is the rich (as well as others) have essentially decided to ignore how children pay the price for the growing emphasis on individualism and personal fulfillment in American society.

The problems of poor children begin early and continue through adulthood. These children will invariably fail to develop their full potential. Instead, they are much more likely to have emotional problems, fail academically, drop out of school, be unemployed, become addicted to drugs, become violent, to join gangs in a search for male authority and a sense of belonging, commit crimes, end up in prison, be on welfare, fail to achieve intimacy in relationships, fail to hold a steady job, fail to form a stable marriage, and have children out of wedlock. Girls growing up in fatherless homes are nearly three times as likely to have an illegitimate child as those in intact families. Most of these poor children are born to single mothers who are poorly educated and unable to provide for themselves or their children.

Most often these poor children are fatherless. David Blankenhorn, the social historian, has said that never before have so many children grown up without knowing what it means to have a father.22 Some

40 percent of all children now live apart from their biological fathers resulting from high divorce rates and unmarried childbearing. Fathers are critical in the establishment of stronger sexual identity and character in both boys and girls. Fatherlessness is also the most important predictor of juvenile crime. Teenagers are now committing 1 of every 3 violent crimes. Of the juveniles in long-term correctional facilities, approximately 70 percent did not live with their fathers while growing up. Approximately 80 percent of those who commit crime grew up in single-parent families. Five out of six prisoners in Hawaii had no father. As a result of the increasing population of juveniles, crime is likely to worsen in the years ahead and the crime rate may explode in the next decade. The tremendous increase in juvenile crime portend future crime and violence at unprecedented levels.

Thirty-two years ago, Senator Daniel Patrick Moynihan wrote:

> From the wild Irish slums of the nineteenth century eastern seaboard, to the riot-torn suburbs of Los Angeles, there is one unmistakable lesson in American history: a community that allows a large number of young men to grow up in broken families, dominated by women, never acquiring any stable relationship to male authority, never acquiring any set of rational expectations about the future—that community asks for and gets chaos. Crime, violence, unrest, disorder—most particularly the furious, unrestrained lashing out at the whole social structure—that is not only to be expected; it is very near to inevitable. And it is richly deserved.23

The consequences of this human tragedy in child welfare will be widening inequality, more immorality, more crime, family breakup, the devastation of the nation's legal and economic systems, and chaos. Values and the weakness of the family are at the heart of the nation's lost generation.

The New Morality

John A. Howard, the Rockford Institute scholar, has noted that decency, morality, lawfulness were once commonly accepted patterns for living in America. They described behavior that was a part of American culture and expected of its people. Their importance and their benefits were taken for granted in America. He points out that what people believe, what they cherish, what they will sacrifice for, what they regard as trivial are the influences that shape the destiny of a nation.24

However, as the cultural analyst Michael Blonsky observes, many people today are totally unpersuaded by any system of beliefs. Blonsky sees the key values of a "New Culture" as ownership of impressive things, glamour, fitness, youth, power, freedom, eroticism, and violence. He says flashy shoes are as important as anything gets for many people today. He sees people as being produced differently than before World War II.25

Derek Bok, the former president of Harvard University, argues that when college students began to feel that it was important to be very well off financially (rose from 41 percent in 1968 to 74 percent in 1995) and that developing a meaningful philosophy of life was not a top priority (fell from 83 percent in 1968 to 41 percent in 1995), personal satisfaction took precedency over a willingness to deal with other people. This change also came with an explosion in divorce, a rise in crime, and other antisocial behaviors.26

Today a "new morality" does govern America and it is reflected in its citizen's focus on self-fulfillment and their selfishness and lack of caring. Today, there is an enormous amount of hedonism in society. Everything has become relative and subjective. Old values and absolutes of good and bad are being discarded and branded as foolish traditions, or as old fashion. Today, no judgments are made on people's behavior because there is no standard of right and wrong that can be brought to bear on their behavior. All bad actions are viewed as nobody's fault, and everything is excusable on one basis or another. Truth and goodness are constantly redefined. There is no judgment of wrong behavior or, at least, rarely is it done. People no longer see truths and morality as universal and unchanging. Instead, they match their values to their behavior. As a society continues to give license to immoral lifestyles by claiming they are new, liberating, or modern, they are at the same time allowing spirituality, morality, and society to die. As the theologian Neal A. Maxwell has said, "A society which permits anything will eventually lose everything."27

One outside observer of this change in America is the Russian writer Alexander Solzhenitsyn who made the statement:

The West ... has been undergoing an erosion and obscuring of high moral and ethical ideals. The spiritual axis of life has grown dim.28

The sociologist Daniel Bell has also said that the lack of a moral belief system presents the deepest challenge to a society's survival.29

Moral decay is evident in the promiscuity of young people, in the easy breakup of marriages, in the infidelity of husbands and wives, in youth gangs, in the increased use of drugs and alcohol, in the epidemic spread of STDs (sexually transmitted diseases) and AIDS, in the disregard for the lives and property of others, and in the breakdown of law and order. Other manifestations of this decay are the endless sex and violence in television, motion pictures, music, modern literature, and the Internet, and their influence on human behavior. All of these evidences, and others, are symptoms of a major crisis of the spirit that permeates the entire American society. Much of this decay is because parents abdicated a higher vision and turned away from a higher power and nation, to themselves and their own comforts, and oftentimes, to the prosperity and freedom they gave to their children.

As long as America continues to focus more on material success and selfish desires, it is unlikely that a moral and spiritual decline will change. America's social crisis will not be solved, or even addressed, until it is fully recognized, and the members of society resolve to change.

How Did America Get to Such a State of Decline?

But, how did America get to such a state? To provide an answer to this most important question requires an understanding of how the world works. This understanding is described in the next six chapters.

Chapter 4

The Universal Social Principles of Life

It was the Greek philosophers who first conceived of the universe as governed by constant and impersonal laws. In trying to discover the laws of the universe, these philosophers assumed that those laws were in fact constant and were understandable. They assumed that there was an ideal, perfect, and orderly universe, and if its rules could be discovered, then every action could be predicted.

Science also assumes the universe or nature is lawful. Human beings and human societies are part of nature, and therefore, are governed by a set of natural laws. In other words, they are subject to regularities that can be isolated and classified, understood, and predicted. The purpose of science is to discover and understand these natural laws or principles. These natural laws explain how the events occurring in nature are caused by other occurring natural events, that is, how human events are caused by social and physical causes. Simply put, they tell us what will happen if we do something.

Some modern-day sociologists say there are no natural laws. Other sociologists recognize there are such laws or principles, but believe that their discovery is not possible, or must continue to await a variety of prior activities. None of these positions are true since these laws have already been discovered, and they do not require any other prior activities. Even though the social sciences have not produced anything resembling a natural law, all social life operates under universal social laws. Humanity has always benefited from compliance with these true principles. All we have to do is describe and understand these laws, and then, consistently follow them for the predicted outcomes. This is within the reach of all humanity today, just as it was in the past. There is already sufficient evidence available to identify these principles.

Laws and Their Types

What are laws? Laws or principles may be defined as the observed regularity of nature. They should have a predictable relationship between two or more variables. This means that laws consist of variables or things, such as the amount of love or socioeconomic status that can vary in amount. These variables are normally related to each other in a cause and effect relationship, where one variable such as person's diet, the causal variable, causes a predictable change in the other variable such as a person's health, the effect variable. In other words, if a change occurs in the causal variable then a change will occur in the effect variable—poor diet results in poor health. They should also be general and universal. Laws are abstract or general, meaning they apply to many specific situations and not to just one specific situation, and are universal or true in all situations, in all time periods, and in all cultures.

There are two major types of laws. The first type of laws, or principles, are those often referred to as the "laws of nature." These laws govern all things in the universe, and always operate the same. They are immutable. These laws have always existed, even though humanity may not be aware of them. These laws do not cease to operate just because we do not recognize them. These laws cannot be changed or circumvented. These laws are self-enforcing. They cannot be overruled by humanity. Much of the suffering that comes to people in life is the result of making choices that are not in harmony with these laws.

The laws of nature may be divided into: universal physical laws and universal social laws. The application of science in the fields of biology, physics, and chemistry attempt to identify universal physical laws, or the natural laws in the physical world, whereas the application of science in the fields of psychology, history, economics, political science, anthropology, and sociology, attempt to identify the universal social laws, or natural laws in the social world.

The other major type of laws are referred to as the "laws of man."

Every society develops social norms, or beliefs, in its culture that tell people what they should do, and not do. Often these rules of behavior are derived from the values in a society. Laws are norms that are formally enacted by the state or government. A law usually carries a defined punishment for its violation. These are laws that are enacted by societies to govern the earthly affairs of their citizens. All governments have a right to make laws, and administer them for the good and safety of society. However, these laws can be changed, and overruled, by humanity. They are no better than the people who write and administer them.

The universal social laws, or principles, are the basis for this explanation of humanity. They are the topic of this chapter. The description of the major universal social laws is done at three different interrelating levels of social activity, because every law is specific to each level and social phenomenon, and has certain conditions. These levels of social activity or analysis are referred to as the micro level, meso level, and macro level. Micro means small. At this level is the individual and the self. At the meso, or middle level, is the web of social relationships that connects the micro level with the macro level. Macro means large, and on this level of activity is an entire society. These divisions are being used to make it easier to understand what will come later as illustrations of how these laws operate within the context of social life.

Universal Social Laws or Principles at the Micro Level

All individuals are bound by universal social laws. Probably the most basic of these laws is the *Law of Opposition*. Human growth and development involves encounters with different life events, trials, or problems requiring people to make choices among alternative actions. There is opposition found in all social life.

The *Law of Opposition* states that opposition in social life leads to different choices in social actions.

This law suggests that people will encounter resistance in life. This law says that humanity can experience such things as good, virtue, success, appreciation for well-being, and happiness as well as bad, corruption, failure, sickness and pain, and sorrow. It also suggests, if people can rise to the highest levels, they can also sink to the lowest levels.

Another basic social law at the micro level is the *Law of Agency,* which is related to the idea of people being free, active, and self-determining.

> The *Law of Agency* states that agency to choose leads to different choices of social action and various degrees of agency.

This law suggests that every person has the independence of mind and the free agency to choose their own thoughts and most actions within the social and physical constraints of the world. It is only through the freedom to exercise agency that there can be the highest prospects for human growth and development. Clearly, everyday life, even if a person lives under the worst government, provides choices to everyone, and we are often compelled to choose among different social actions. However, it is also possible that agency can be restricted, or end, when a person makes a choice; for a person does not have the agency to choose the consequences that may take away or limit their ability to exercise further agency. In other words, the agency possessed by any person is increased or diminished by the use to which the person puts it. Most of these choices will take place in the context of other people and the social circumstances of a particular situation as well as in the context of biophysical limitations.

Spirituality is a state of mind. It is a belief in the supernatural and in sacred values. It is a basic philosophy toward life. A spiritual person's behavior conforms to moral, sacred, or religious values. The spirituality of a person determines their values in life.

> The *Law of Spirituality* states a person's level of spirituality determines a person's values in life.

Values play a major role in nearly every theory in the broad realm of social and behavioral sciences, and are a primary cause of social action. Values are ideas of how to live and what people think is good and what is not good in the world. According to the sociologist Tamotsu Shibutani, values tell people "what goals' people ought to seek, what is required or forbidden, what is honorable and shameful, and what is beautiful and ugly."1 Simply put, values or desires shape social behavior. The choices' people make in life, and what they seek in life, are determined by their personal values and emotions. These values are found in the mind of a person, and have been learned and accepted by the person. These values make people what they are, and largely determine their morals and the kind of lives people will live. It is these basic values that determine a person's motivations and priorities in life, and their purpose in life.

The *Law of Values* states personal values shape a person's motives.

It is values that shape and motivate people as well as determine their thoughts in life.

The *Law of Motivations* states a person's motives shape a person's thoughts.

We become as well as do what we think. Thoughts are energy, and may be perceived as something akin to magnets that attract us to the various things we think. The choices that people make, and the social actions in their lives, are a product of their thoughts. In other words, people's actions are reflections from the thoughts of their minds, or from what is often called "the inner person," even though it is possible for a person's actions to be based on wrong reasons. Choices and social actions are preceded primarily by non-rational thoughts based on personal values and emotions and personal perceptions of social reality. This is stated in a law of action.

The *Law of Action* states social action is determined by a person's thoughts.

For every social action taken by an individual there is some social consequence. These consequences may be beneficial or detrimental to the individual, depending on the type of social action that has occurred. Bad actions always have destructive and detrimental consequences, and this is true not only for the individual but also for society. This law is similar to the "law of the harvest" found in the *Bible*, which states that "whatsoever a man soweth, that shall he also reap" (Gal. 6:7).

The *Law of Consequences* states for every social action there is a consequence.

Closely related to the Law of Action and the Law of Consequences is a law formulated by the author and behavioralist Richard W.

Wetherill (1906-1989) as the "law of absolute right." The law states that right action gets right results, whereas wrong action gets wrong results.2

The *Law of Action* and the *Law of Consequences* are also similar to the Swedish philosopher Emil F. Smidak's Principle of Action and Re-Action where "action" comprises activities, forces, and influences as well as thoughts, words, expressions, gestures, etc., and "re-action" signifies response, counter-effect, and consequence, etc.3

Universal Social Laws or Principles at the Meso Level

All human beings are social in nature. This simply means that humans need others for their survival. The nature of the human being requires two unique qualities. First, we are social in that our lives are linked to others and society in many complex ways. Second, we are cultural in that what we become is not a result of instinct, but of ideas, values, and rules developed in society. People would not be what they are if it were not for these two unique qualities. That human beings are social beings is an accepted fact among the social sciences.

Each person depends on the well-being of the whole planet Earth, and its various inhabitants. More specific to the social world, all people develop as social beings through a process of social interaction with other people. In other words, people need each other if they are to develop as individuals. Everyone in the human family owes much to everyone else because every person's growth and development, and support, is wholly interdependent upon others. If one person fails, it will affect every other person, particularly those persons in the failing person's immediate social network, such as family and close friends.

Actually, the world can be viewed as a "sea of humanity," with every person affecting everyone else, and when they are all lifting each other simultaneously, they are all better off because people are experiencing success and growth. However, if people are tearing each other down, then they suffer and fail in the "sea of humanity," whether they realize it or not. Like it or not, each person is constantly exerting a force on every other person, as well as, being acted upon by others. The level of the "sea of humanity" can only rise to the level of the growth experienced by its membership. People can help other people grow and develop by eliminating their stumbling blocks, encouraging them, by being an example, by not speaking evilly of them, by not judging and being critical, and by understanding their imperfections. Groups, particularly the family, are very important as each person continues to progress as social beings. This is stated in the *Law of Social Growth.*

The *Law of Social Growth* states social interaction and life events lead to individual social growth and development.

What a person learns as they experience social growth and development through social interaction with others and life events will influence their future social behavior. Because people can learn new things from experiences as well as from their predecessors and remember those things they learn, their progress is cumulative. Social learning, particularly in the early years or formative years of a person's life, is vitally important for determining a person's sense of self throughout life and for determining the future behavior of the individual. Critical in this learning or socializing process, is the family, the social unit that has the primary responsibility for socializing as well as the most influence on new members in society.

The *Law of Social Learning* states social learning influences the future behavior of persons.

Societies are made up of interacting individuals. In other words, it is through a web or network of social relationships between individuals, who are interacting and communicating, that societies develop and operate. Societies, in turn, help shape the individuals who belong to them. Another law at the meso level focuses on the primary ingredient of this level of social activity, social interaction.

The *Law of Social Interaction* states social interaction is determined by individual values and perceptions of social reality through ongoing interaction between individuals.

This law suggests people act according to the way they define the situation they find themselves in and by the other people they interact with. The sociologist, W. I. Thomas (1863-1947), made the related observation that situations that are defined as real are real in their consequences. That is, people's actions and behaviors are based on how they perceive a social situation or social reality. This observation is known as the Thomas theorem.[4] The term social reality would also include our values, emotions, motivations, and thoughts, which are influenced by our accumulated experiences and perceptions of reality.

As individuals socially interact with one another they will tend to mingle with, and form friendships with, those who are similar to themselves. Most important in this process is the similarity of values that these people share. Eventually in stratified societies the rich ignore the poor, pretending they just do not exist.

> The *Law of Association* states the more people agree in values, the greater the probability they will associate with one another.

Prophets, poets, and thinkers of every age have declared love as the most important of all the virtues. Loving others is at the core of humanity. This is also what near-death researchers have learned from the spiritual evidence gathered from those who have experienced near death and a near-death experience. As the saying goes, it is love that makes the world go round. The editor David Lawrence (1888-1973) wrote, "For the principle of love is not merely affection for each other. It connotes tolerance, helpfulness, willingness to share each other's resources and, above all, rendering unto others the respect and the consideration that equals deserve from one another."5 Probably the greatest love comes when we are kind to each other. This requires people be considerate, complimentary, charitable, and grateful. This principle is what some have called the "Golden Rule." This rule states: Do to others as you would be done by (based on Matthew 7:12). Charity is exemplified when we are as concerned about the well-being of others as much as our own. People must also give love if they are to receive it, as stipulated in the *Law of Restoration* later. Love requires acts of love. A line from William Shakespeare's play, "The Two Gentlemen of Verona," says people do not love if they do not show their love.6 This important principle is reflected in the next law.

> The *Law of Charity* states the more people act in unconditional loving ways toward each other the more peaceful is social life, and the less they act in these ways the more conflict in social life.

The opposite of people acting in unconditional loving ways toward each other, of course, is people acting in hateful ways. This results in more conflict in social life.

A psychologist named Morton Deutsch developed what he called a "law of human behavior."7 A considerable amount of research supports this law. This law suggests that others would tend to act the same way around persons as they act around them. In other words, how a person acts tends to create the same behavior in those around them. If, for example, a person competes with someone else for wealth and position, they tend to compete too. If a person uses force against someone, this will cause more force. This law is very similar to the commonly used saying, "What goes around comes around."

This law of human behavior has two different parts according to Deutsch. One part is the ripple effect of the law that suggests that a person's actions tend to be spread out around them much like throwing a pebble in a pond. The other part of the law could be called the restoration effect of the law. This part suggests that the actions that spread out from a person also tend to come back to them.

The illustrator Florence Scovel Shinn stated it this way: "The Game of Life is a game of boomerangs. Man's thoughts, deeds and words, return to him sooner or later, with astounding accuracy."8 This law is restated below in a law of restoration.

The *Law of Restoration* states the social actions of people toward other people result in those actions being restored to them.

Finally, at the meso level is another law: the *Law of Stratified Social Relations*. This law pertains particularly to the social relationships in highly stratified or unequal societies. These are societies that display high levels of inequality between their members. These societies often have a small group of people who are rich and a large group of people who are poor with few people in between these two groups. The relationships in these societies become distrustful because their relationships are based on getting personal gain at any cost.

The *Law of Stratified Social Relations* states the materialistic and opportunistic motives for social relations in stratified societies lead to the breakdown of these relationships and social order.

Universal Social Laws or Principles at the Macro Level

It is only through the social interaction of people who are doing things with one another in various institutions, organizations, and other groups that a society is possible. The people in any society develop certain social patterns through the course of their social interaction that eventually results in a history, a culture, a language, and an identity that they share. Societies are shaped by the individuals who belong to them, and they in turn, are largely shaped by their families. The family is the greatest social group and institution in the history of humankind. It is good and strong families that are the best source of good people and good societies. The first law at the macro level focuses on family.

The *Law of Family* states the spiritual strength of families determines the well-being of a society.

The second law at the macro level focuses primarily on the material resources or wealth of a society. The material resources of any society, such as food, clothing, and shelter, are the result of the labor by its membership.

The *Law of Work* states human labor leads to the production of the resources in a society.

Societies determine how their resources will be distributed among their memberships. The distributive or economic system of a society is vitally important for determining the structure of the society. Generally, if these resources are equitably distributed, there is little or no stratification or division of society into social strata, and a stable society tends to develop. There are less or no poor members in this society. However, if the resources of a society are inequitably distributed, then there is stratification and society will be divided into different social strata or classes. It is then that an unequal or stratified society develops.

The *Law of Shared Resources* states a society that equitably distributes its resources to all its members generally leads to equality among its membership.

The next law points to the fact in life that there are poor people, or people who live in poverty in societies. Their circumstances can be altered only by the economic system of society. Such a system will be described later in this book.

The *Law of the Poor* states the number of poor people in a society varies with the economic system of the society.

Whether a society equitably distributes its resources or not to its members, will not only determine the amount of poverty and equality among its membership, but also the amount of satisfaction, harmony, morality, and prosperity experienced by its people.

The *Law of Compliance and Collective Consequence* states the more a society is in harmony with the *Law of Shared Resources*, the more it experiences happiness, peace, morality, equality, and prosperity, and the more a society is incongruous with the *Law of Shared Resources,* the more it experiences unhappiness, conflict, immorality, inequality, and suffering.

The course of a society's development is determined by the spirituality and social values of its collective membership. History has recorded that those civilizations that have established a central belief and value system, have experienced the greatest progress. These social values are based on the society's ideas of how to live and say what general goals ought to be sought by a society. They provide the broad guidelines for social behavior in a society. All societies are guided by their spirituality and a set of core values, or desires, of its citizens.

The *Law of Collective Spirituality* states the spirituality of a society determine its collective values.

The *Law of Collective Values* states the social values of a society determine the motivations and strivings of its collective membership.

The core values of a society may vary over the course of time. These values are commitments, and they reflect what is considered good and what is considered not good in society. Some examples of core values are freedom, equality, individualism, making a lot of money, progress, and so on. Whatever the core values of a society may be, they do influence the path and direction society takes. The collective social actions of a people in a society are a result of the society's collective values and motivations. This is stated in the next law.

The *Law of Collective Action* states the collective social action of a society's membership is determined by their collective motivation.

The core values of society determine the direction of society as well as the social organization of society. When many people act in a similar way as they carry out various pursuits that are guided by the values of society, they produce a cumulative effect on society and on its different institutions, or major activities. This causes changes in society that can alter every aspect of the lives of its members, from education to religion, to government, to economy, and to family. These changes are far-reaching, general developments that can affect all the various social patterns, particularly the economic patterns, found in society. They set an almost irreversible direction for society.

The *Law of Social Change* states the spiritual or material pursuits by the members of a society change the social structure of society.

One value that distinguishes between stable and stratified societies is materialism. People will always have a propensity for material goods in a society. When the priorities of the membership in a society are fixed on the acquisition, use, and/or possession of things, such as property or wealth, we call this condition "materialism." With the inequitable acquisition of wealth comes the feeling of superiority that makes people status-conscious. Wealth gives status or prestige as well as power to those who possess it. In a materialistic society, wealth becomes the measure of success.

The *Law of Materialism* states materialistic values lead to members of a society working for wealth, power, and prestige.

Once the members of society value materialistic pursuits and material well-being, they begin to compete for wealth, power, and prestige. Those who are more successful in acquiring wealth, power, and prestige, will have access to more of the resources and pleasures in society than those who are less successful. This materialistic behavior causes inequality among the membership of a society. As a result, society becomes stratified and divides into classes, each having their class-based interests. Some of the classes are dominated by others as they now begin competing with each other for wealth, power, and prestige, and the plentiful but finite resources of society.

The *Law of Division* states the inequitable distribution of resources in a society leads to the division of society into classes of people.

Social inequality is the basic cause of social conflict in society, and even intense conflict, which may eventually destroy society.

The *Law of Inequality* states the more social inequality in a society, the more conflict and destruction of the social and moral fabric in society.

Immorality is the infallible attendant of economic inequality. All immoral behavior impacts on society, even innocent people are affected. It involves such things as honesty, integrity, justice, and responsibility as well as sexual behavior. As material pursuits prevail in society, the relevance of moral values declines and the moral fiber of society declines. The desire for wealth, and/or the love of money, causes selfishness, envy, arrogance, greed, dishonesty, crime, corruption, hatred, war, distrust, immoral lifestyles, obscenity, and a host of other social evils, such as violence in society. For example, the social researchers James Patterson and Peter Kim's found that Americans would do almost anything, including lie, cheat, steal, murder, abandon their families, and change their religion, for a fistful of dollars.9 In other words, with the recognition of the all-importance of wealth, any morals that may stand in the way of its acquisition, are pushed aside to the point of bearing false witness, stealing, plundering, and even murder being permissible, as long as a person is not caught. The strength of society is no more, or less, than the moral strength of the members of society. No nation or civilization can endure for very long without moral strength in the homes and lives of its people.

The *Law of Morality* states the more the materialism and economic inequality in a society, the more the selfishness and immorality in society.

The recognition of these major universal social laws allows us now to begin making social things in the world understandable and causally explaining and predicting social phenomena. However, this is not to say that there are not other universal social principles, but only that those that are most crucial for understanding and explaining the social world have been mentioned and described.

Chapter 5

The Spiritual Factor: The Forgotten Factor and Determinant of Societal and Personal Destiny

The best predictor of a person's attitudes and behavior is the spirituality of the individual. It is the spirituality of a society's members that determines the spirituality of the nation. It is the spiritual strengths of a people that knit together the very fabric of a society and determine its fate. The greatest nations were made great by instilling within its citizens the highest spiritual values. If people are to understand what happens to people and societies, it is absolutely necessary to understand the concept of spirituality. A complete picture and total explanation of the world is only possible with the consideration of this mostly ignored dimension of reality. No attempt to explain humanity will ever be complete without the inclusion of the spiritual factor.

Today, we continuously hear from religious leaders, scholars, activists, political theorists, and others of the enormous spiritual crisis in American society. The products of wealth, technology, and science have failed to satisfy the inner spiritual hungering of people, or to have contributed to their spiritual development. Widespread materialism, cynicism, and the capitalist ethic of self-interest has left people unhappy, and searching for meaning. This recognition by so many has raised the question of whether religious principles are essential for a good society. The historians Will (1885-1991) and Ariel Durant have said that there is not one significant example in history where a society was able to maintain a moral life without the help of religion.1 Yet, as a whole, academicians and scientists, who for the most part do not believe in a god, have tended to ignore the religious influence on life.

Americans, as well as, members of other industrial societies, are mostly ignorant of spirituality and the spiritual dimension, of its significance in history and in other civilizations, and of its significance in contemporary society. This is a dimension that has been ignored too long in our quest to understand society and the world.

The Role of Spirituality in Society

Society's cultural tradition is constituted by the meanings of a religious system of beliefs. It is the heart and foundation of a culture, and what holds a society together. Religious based concepts of reality have been the backbone upon which entire cultures have been based. Spiritual principles have made contributions to philosophy and literature, to the development of familial, educational, governmental, and political institutions, and to the mores of societies. These principles underlie the very legal and moral systems of societies. The very foundations of Judeo-Christian secular law is the Ten Commandments. This secular law is the basis of law, particularly in Western civilization, and still undergrids America's system of self-government.

Research has shown that religion is also an important factor in the lives of many people today. Research shows that highly religious people are healthier, less distressed, find meaning and life satisfaction, make better psychological adjustments and experience better emotional well being, avoid drugs and crime, have lower mortality rates and recover quicker from medical illnesses, and have stronger marriages and families. Studies around the world also show that very spiritual people report being very happy.

However, with every passing decade recently, it appears that the world has become ever more spiritually impoverished. America seems lost to a spiritual malaise too. This is particularly evident in the research findings of James Patterson and Peter Kim, who found that only 13 percent of Americans believe in all of the Ten

Commandments, and that America lacks any moral consensus.2 Today, society lacks the spiritual base that holds society together and provides an explanation for the meaning of life.

Definition of Spirituality

What is this most important factor that so strongly influences the behavior of individuals and nations? It is the factor of "spirituality" or the spiritual factor. Spirituality is a strong belief in the supernatural and sacred values that leads to a conscious conception of how to live life and a distinctive desire to live that particular pattern of life. This definition of spirituality suggests first that spirituality is a state of mind. What people believe about the nature of man, the universe, and a supreme being or beings, affects their social behavior. Second, it suggests that a person's state of mind combines with a desire for a particular conception of life. Third, the definition suggests a distinctive desire to live this conception of life. And fourth, it suggests that spirituality is related to a person's thoughts that will eventually shape their actions and makes the person what he or she is. This distinctive desire that shapes a person's motives is also the one that identifies his or her purpose in life.3

Who is a Spiritual Person?

The degree of spirituality of a person is evident in their behavior or actions and what they seek in life. History reveals that through the ages men of high achievement have been motivated by good desires while in their youth. A deeply spiritual person is one who is charitable, compassionate, full of love, gentle, happy, humble, kind, merciful, meek, patient, selfless, submissive, and virtuous. This is a person who is happy when others succeed, concerned for others, helps others, has no mind to injure others, is just to others, loves others, and serves others, particularly the needy. Humble behavior is evidence of spiritual strength even though some see it as a sign of weakness.

The opposite to spirituality is materialism and the pride it engenders. A deeply unspiritual or material person is one who gives priority to material needs and things. This person is the opposite of a spiritual person and tends to be angry, arrogant, envious, greedy, lustful, proud, selfish, unhappy, and violent. These people are sometimes referred to as people without civilization, or without principle. Of course, there are different degrees of spirituality and materialism between spiritual and unspiritual persons. It should also be understood that there is nothing inherently evil about money. What is really critical here is the degree of spiritually and the attitude a person has as they view and manage the things of the world. Nevertheless, it is the desires of materialism or spirituality that guide the thoughts which shape people's actions and make people what they are. It is a person's most deeply held desires that govern their choices in life. Eventually, a person's life adds up to what he or she really wants or desires.

The desires or qualities called materialism and spirituality are expressive of the priorities and attitudes toward the nature and purpose of life. Eventually, a person's level of spirituality, his or her true desire, will become an integral part of himself or herself.

The Importance of Religious Values

Everything cultural from family to government rests upon ideas. The sociologist Robert Nisbet points out that various individuals have been responsible for more history than multitudes have or ever will. The power of these persons rests upon revolutions in ideas and idea systems.4 The importance of religious values for a society is demonstrated in the classic work of Max Weber. His work showed it is the nature of ideas—that is, people's values or desires and beliefs—which initiated industrialization. He argued that major changes could not have occurred without ideas. In his classic sociological essay entitled, *The Protestant Ethic and the Spirit of Capitalism*, he showed how religious beliefs, or the "Protestant Ethic," encouraged hard work, the accumulation of capital, and other activities that brought about industrial capitalism in the 1700s. These Protestant beliefs emphasized thrift, worldly activity, and efforts to attain success. He also found that the religious beliefs of China, and other Eastern religions, emphasized harmony with, and passivity to, the forces of nature and the world. As a result of this belief system, there was no development of capitalism in those societies of the time.5

Secularization and the Influence of Religion

More recently in history, the spread of industrialization and urbanization in the world has lead to a heavy reliance on science and technology—the physical or material world. This transition from traditional and stable to modern and stratified societies has been marked by a process referred to as "secularization." Secularization refers to the declining influence of religion on the world. Secularization is a focus on this world, and on reason, science, and technology, to solve problems as opposed to unquestioned faith and a focus on the next world. Science says there is no next world and that with death comes the end of a man and woman, a philosophy referred to as "naturalism." The secular spirit of secularization is marked by an emphasis on material consumption and a focus on the individual rather than the community. Sociologists generally agree that the influence of religion in the modern world is declining.

It was near the end of the nineteenth century that the German philosopher Friedrich Nietzsche (1844-1900) announced, "God is dead!"6 Nietzsche argued that religion used to be the basis for a sense of purpose and meaning in life. But now, according to Nietzsche, men will have to create their own values and get use to what he called "the loneliness of being." He said they should now understand that life is without purpose, and that there is no superior entities watching over the fate of people. Today, in academic and intellectual circles at least, Nietzsche is almost unanimously regarded as one of the philosophical giants of modern times.

Bible scholars, anthropologists, psychologists, and sociologists have also invented the idea that religion evolved. Most sociologists of religion have dealt with religion as though it were a manmade myth. For example, the French sociologist, Emile Durkheim (1855-1917), believed religion provided a mirror for members of society to see their common unity through sacred symbols, and that through religious rituals, people were actually worshiping society or themselves.7 In other words, the worship of God is seen as a barely disguised worship of society. Karl Marx (1818-1883), the German sociologist, said that religion was created by humans and is managed by the ruling classes to justify their economic, political, and social advantage over the oppressed.8 Thus, religion is nothing more than a creation of the human mind. Since the splitting of the social sciences from religion during the Renaissance, the social sciences have played down religion's importance in the scheme of things. Two exceptions to this trend have been Max Weber, who stated that history and culture are influenced by spiritual as well as material forces, and the sociologist Robert Bellah, who takes seriously the idea that God is real and acts in the lives of human beings and modern nations.9

A new faith has arisen in the ability of "reason" to solve all of our human problems, including our human need for moral guidance. However, reason or rationalism has been unable to develop a compelling, self-justifying moral code. Over the past 30 years, as modern societies have continued to grope for a moral code, there has been a repudiation of rationalism in favor of what is called "moral relativism." According to relativism, what is right is what you believe is right—right and wrong are relative to the individual's own beliefs and standards. Relativism says everybody has to find his or her own values in their own time, and since there is nothing right or wrong, there are no absolutes. In other words, with moral relativism, society lacks absolute standards of right and wrong—a standardless society.

Standardless societies forget the costly lessons of history because they tend to focus upon things like "me" and "now," and not on a history out of which to fashion a future. History discloses that in era after era of time, the same or similar difficulties and problems of today have been met. History also discloses that for the most part, history is the history of the human mind or ideas, ideas that have shaped the course of humanity. The German philosopher Frederick Hegel (1770-1831) once made a statement to the effect that those who do not learn from history will have to repeat it.10 The Spanish poet and philosopher George Santayana (1863-1952) made a similar statement when he said, "Those who cannot remember the past are condemned to repeat it." 11 That is exactly what humanity has done century after century. Today, it seems people are no different from those who proceeded them in understanding history. There is no future for a standardless society, which eventually imprisons its membership much as unlicensed actions will eventually imprison an individual. And, once basic moral standards are removed, tolerance changes into permissiveness.

History tends to confirm that a society that permits anything eventually looses everything. But, maybe even more important, is that these different ideas, beliefs, and values cause different behaviors and consequences. As Christopher Booker has said:

> When men cease to aspire to the ideal, the good, to self-restraint—whether in their hearts or in their lives—they do not just stand still, but actually turn the other way, finding self-fulfillment in self-indulgence, and in ... those three ultimate expressions of the totally self centered life: sex, violence, and insanity.12

There is no ultimate purpose outside oneself. The object of life is simply the pursuit of individual pleasure.

In postindustrial societies, the belief based on relativism and Nietzsche's work that everything is permitted since God is dead seems to have become the dominant moral code. In other words, anything goes and there is essentially no moral basis or meaning for society. Certainly today, there tends to be a heavy reliance on the secular world for moral direction, compared to the past, when there was a heavy reliance on the sacred and a higher power. According to the legal professor Stephen Carter, this is due in part because the American elite and the media has promoted the view that religion is backward, medieval, and irrelevant.13 The courts have also vigorously promoted secularity in all public functions.

Most people in America believe religion is in decline, even though they believe religion can answer all or most of today's problems, according to *Religion in America 1992-93* by pollster George Gallup Jr. Gallup's work suggests that intellectuals may be correct when they talk about an amoral code in society. Gallup pointed out in his 1990 report on religion that there is an ethics gap or difference in America between the way people think of themselves and the way they really are. George Barna's *Barna Report 1992-93* also indicates an acceptance of moral relativism and a lack of intense pursuit of faith in the United States. These findings suggest Americans, who have been described as living in one of the most religious countries in the Christian world, are not really practicing their religious beliefs.

The legal scholar Robert Bork makes the following statement based on recent findings from sociological surveys:

> The truth is that, despite the statistics on churchgoing, etc., the United States is a very secular nation that, for the most part, does not take religion seriously. Not only may the statistics overstate religious reality—people may be telling pollsters what they think makes a good impression—but statistics say nothing of the quality or depth of American religious belief. It is increasingly clear that very few people who claim a religion could truthfully say that it informs their attitudes and significantly affects their behavior.14

Large segments of American society seem to be turning away from God and consider Him irrelevant or declare Him dead. This is contrary to a recent book, *One Nation, After All* by the sociologist Alan Wolfe, who tells us based on his talks with people in eight communities in America, that a central value in the lives of most people is God.

It is important to realize, however, that this process of secularization is not peculiar to modern times, but has occurred in cycles throughout the history of humanity as societies have moved back and forth between spirituality and materialism. At the end of the 18th century, almost every thinker predicted religion would disappear by the 20th century. Yet religion, one manifestation of spirituality, in some form appears strong and viable in most countries of the world. Today, sociologists, and other scholars, are beginning to challenge the assumption that scientific thought and modern technology will replace religion, and are resuming serious study of religion again. In actuality, religious transformation runs in cycles. Throughout history the renewal and reform of religion, and the falling away from religion, have been repeated over and over again.

As the author Irving Kristol said,

It is crucial in the lives of all our citizens, as it is to all human beings at all times, that they encounter a world that possesses a transcendent meaning, a world in which the human experience makes sense. Nothing is more dehumanizing, more certain to generate a crisis, than to experience one's life as a meaningless event in a meaningless world.15

A similar feeling is expressed by Bellah who says,

Every nation finds its legitimacy in being a part of a larger context. The cosmos, the movement of history, or the purposes of God, provide the nation with its reasons for being. Society is never merely a social contract, an association of individuals who band together out of mutual self-interest. It always transcends the social and finds its meaning in the sacred.16

The social analysts Gabriel Almond, Marvin Chodorov, and Ray Harvey Pearce suggest the troubles in America stem from the disappearance of the core of sacred beliefs and the lack of belief in something greater than the life immediately around us, which has always been at the center of any genuine culture.17

The sociologists James Duke and Barry Johnson have found that generally people tend to turn to religion when they are in trouble and in dire situations. Religion gives meaning to existence and serves as an anchor in people's lives when they experience political and economic suppression and exploitation. In turn, they have found that most people turn away from religion, and that the greatest degree of secularization are found in societies where life is easier and political and economic rights are guaranteed.18 Robert Bork also points out that "religion tends to be strongest when life is hard, and the same may be said of morality and law."19

The most powerful causal determinant in the world is spirituality. No society can be created or maintained unless it has a spiritual mandate to give meaning to its existence. It is the spirituality (the *Law of Spirituality*) of people that is the cause of the fate of nations and the world.

Chapter 6

The Individual: The Basic Element of Society

The individual has infinite worth, and is the most important and basic element in society. At the heart of democracy and freedom is the belief in the infinite worth of the individual. People are superior to the social structures they create, whether it be a society or the institutions of a society such as the economy, education, family, government, or religion.

However, within sociology, there have been two major views on what should be the unit of primary attention. One view holds it is society and its components that should be the primary focus. The other view is that the behavior of the individual, or the accumulated acts of individuals, should be the major focus. It is the accumulated acts of the members of a society who shape the society, even though there is an interacting influence of the collectivities or groups and the accumulated social structure of society on the individual that must be taken into account in understanding the social world.

The Composition of the Individual

What is an individual? The social psychologist, George Herbert Mead (1863-1931), and the Austrian psychoanalyst, Sigmund Freud (1856-1939), both attempted to describe the personality before 1930.1 Mead felt the personality or self was composed of two parts: the "me" and the "I." He said the "I" is the conscious, spontaneous, and creative part of the self, and the "me" the part of the self defined by other people and the social group. The "me" is a product of socialization and social interaction with other people. The self or personality was separate from the body according to Mead.

Freud visualized the self or personality as composed of three parts: the "id," the "superego," and the "ego." He said the "id" consists of the biological drives or instinctive desires, urges, and impulses that human beings inherit. The "superego" is the conscience and represents society's norms and moral values as learned primarily from parents. The "ego" is the rational or conscious aspect of the personality that seeks to satisfy the impulses of the id in a socially acceptable way. Freud saw these parts as processes operating within a person's mind.

These explanations of personality or self do not, however, provide a complete and accurate understanding of the individual. Only recently has science acquired information from near-death research that allows for a fuller understanding of what makes up an individual.

This research indicates the "person" consists of a physical body and a spirit that has a mind and a spirit body. The "physical body" is coarse matter. It experiences urges and desires and is controlled by the mind. In turn, every thought, word, and action as well as the passage of time affects the physical body.

The "mind" is the conscious and intelligent part of men and women—the part that perceives, feels, wills, and thinks. It is the innermost character of people, and it is words as well as actions that are reflections from the very interior of the mind. As people go through life, their mind reasons, wills their actions, and takes in whatever they receive and stores it. The mind is a complete record of a person's experiences, and it is the sum of a person's thoughts and actions that shapes the character of their spirits. As William James (1842-1910), the psychologist and philosopher, said, "The mind is made up by what it feeds upon."2 The mind operates the physical body through what might be described as the body's control center, known as the (physical) brain. It works much like someone operating a puppet, with the mind directing the operation of the physical body through commands to the brain. It is a person's thoughts that control the behavior of their physical body.

The "spirit body" has the same features as the physical body and occupies the physical body during mortality much like a hand in a glove. It is constituted of undetectable refined matter. The mind of a person is in his or her spirit body, and both constitute what may be referred to as the "spirit." The spirit is pure and everlasting energy that is the life force for the physical body and survives physical death.

A "conscience" is part of the individual. The conscience is inborn in the individual from conception and allows every person to know basic right and wrong choices intuitively. Even current research shows that all children develop a moral sense in the second year of life and future research should eventually show, to the extent possible, that the conscience is present from the beginning of life. In fact, we find most peoples of the world possess common values of justice, honesty, respect for life, family life, freedom, work, forgiveness, spirituality, and so on. As a person participates in life's activities, the conscience continually works to enlighten the mind and strives to guide the person in personal choices. However, a person can also choose to ignore or repress the conscience. Whatever a person may choose to do, it is the conscience that makes all people accountable to the laws of humankind, subject only to the quality of the spirit when it comes into the world.

The term "soul" refers to the spirit and the physical body of an individual. Often this term is used in discussions on this topic. It is a term that has been variously defined throughout history, but often used in conjunction with spirit.

The most dominant viewpoint on the soul in the Western world today is that of the French philosopher Rene Descartes (1596-1650). Descartes felt each person had a physical body that was a machine composed of bones, blood, muscles, nerves, and skin controlled by the brain and a soul that was immaterial and immortal. The theory became known as "dualism."3

More recently, the neurologist, Richard Restak concluded that there is no such thing as a soul after his attempts to find it on a PET scanner machine failed.4 However, at the end of his life, Wilder Penfield (1891-1976), the Father of Neurosurgery, wrote:

> Taken either way, the nature of the mind presents the fundamental problem, perhaps the most difficult and most important of all problems. For myself, after a professional lifetime spent in trying to discover how the brain accounts for the mind, it comes as a surprise now to discover, during this final examination of the evidence, that the dualist hypothesis (the mind separate from the brain) seems the more reasonable of explanations.
>
> Since every man must adopt for himself, without the help of science, his way of life and his personal religion, I have long had my own private beliefs. What a thrill it is, then, to discover that the

scientists, too, can legitimately believe in the existence of the spirit!

Possibly the scientist and the physician could add something by stepping outside the laboratory and the consulting room to reconsider these strangely gifted human beings about us. Where did the mind—call it the spirit if you like—come from? Who can say? It exists. The mind is attached to the action of a certain mechanism within the brain. A mind has been thus attached in the case of every human being for many thousands of generations, and there seems to be significant evidence of heredity in the mind's character from one generation to the next and the next. But at present, one can only say simply and without explanation, 'the mind is born.'5

The pediatrician Melvin Morse and his team of researchers, and other researchers, believe they have discovered the seat of the soul and the energy responsible for mind-action in the Sylvian fissure of the right temporal lobe of the brain, located just above the right ear.6

The Origins of the Personality

When does the development of the personality begin? When does a person have a personality? Psychologists say that the development of personality begins at birth and by the age of three our personalities have developed. It was not too long ago, they said that a personality is developed by age six. At one time years ago, some were saying the personality develops by age eight. The fact is a newly born infant already has a personality that continues to change through life.

It is known, based on the work of the psychologist David Chamberlain and others, that unborn and newborn children can learn and remember words said to them prenatally. They can also sense while in the womb whether the mother wants them. In other words, they experience life even while in the mother's womb.7 The psychologist, Carroll Izard, has found that infants display a wide range of emotional expressions on their faces long before they are able to speak. Some of these emotions are even present from birth.8 The psychologist, Judith Langlois, has found that infants prefer attractive human faces, challenging the notion that standards of attractiveness are learned through years of cultural conditioning.9 Rebecca A. Eder, a psychologist, has found that children have a more fully developed self-concept than is generally believed even though they may lack an adult's awareness of having a personality.10 A research team headed by Annette Axtmann found that babies are innately social and can develop special relationships with other infants as young as six weeks.11 What is the meaning of these findings? Certainly they challenge our understanding of personality development.

A few near-death researchers have actually discovered evidence for a life before earth life. 12 This evidence suggests a premortal existence where it is logical to assume that each person developed a personality before birth. This means that the capacities and abilities, desires, inclinations, and aptitudes a person developed in this existence are still a part of him or her as they continue their life on earth. This is further highlighted by the fact that most mothers who have given birth to a child say that almost immediately they recognize an individual personality in a newborn child. The psychologist, Jerome Kagan, whose work has focused on the development of children during their first 10 years of life, suggests that children are born with different initial qualities that influence their development.13

Although many scientists remain unduly closed minded when it comes to near-death research, it has much to offer to our understanding of personality and its development. It is just possible that the earlier work of the psychiatrists, Stanton Samenow and Samuel Yochelson, the sociobiologist, James Q. Wilson, and the psychologist, Richard J. Herrnstein, suggesting that criminals are born is more accurate than they or anyone else might suspect.14 Their work suggests that criminals from early age have personality characteristics and thinking patterns that make them different from non-criminals.

The idea of a premortal existence is not new. Past poets and philosophers spoke of such an existence. For instance, the British poet Henry Vaughn (1622-1695) wrote "The Retreate," a poem recalling a premortal existence.15 Another British poet, William Wordsworth (1770-1850), also wrote about a preexistence in "Intimations of Immorality."16 The Greek philosopher, Socrates, argued in the third century B. C. for a preexistence in one of his dialogues, the *Phaedo:*

> Your favorite doctrine, Socrates, that knowledge is simply recollection, if true, also necessarily implies a previous time in which we have learned that which we now recollect. But this would be impossible unless our soul had been in some place before existing in the form of man; here then is another proof of the soul's immortality.17

In the same book Socrates says, "Our souls must also have existed without bodies before they were in the form of man, and must have had intelligence."18

In *Phaedrus,* Socrates argues the soul is immortal. He says:

> The soul through all her being is immortal, for that which is ever in motion is immortal; but that which moves another and is moved by another, in ceasing to move ceases also to live. Only the self-moving, ever-learning, self never ceases to move and is the fountain and beginning of motion to all that moves besides. Now the beginning is unbegotten, for that which is begotten has a beginning; ... if unbegotten, it must also be indestructible; for if beginning were destroyed, there could be no beginning out of anything, nor anything out of a beginning.... Therefore the self-moving is the beginning of motion; and this can neither be destroyed nor begotten, else the whole heavens and all creation would collapse and stand still, and never again have motion or birth.... That which is moved from within has a soul, for such is the nature of the soul. But if this be true, must not the soul be the self-moving, and therefore of necessity unbegotten and immortal?19

Thomas Traherne (1637?-1674), the English poet and religious writer, felt that this world is a gift granted by a loving God to his child in the life before.20

A new light is shed on human life once people realize the newborn have had a premortal existence, and have a personality. All people are different from one another, with varying interests, inclinations, and talents—some having some abilities and others having different abilities. All people also have different strengths and different degrees of strengths as well as each individual has a lesser or greater propensity for spirituality. On the basis of observations of mortal experience, it is reasonable to assume that there was a variation of development resulting in differences and gradations of individuals before the time of life on earth. The knowledge of premortal existence provides a new understanding on the origins of personality and why each person is different and has a unique personality.

A personality is the sum of its character which distinguishes a person from all others. A person's character is developed by their thoughts. Benjamin Disraeli (1804-1881), Prime Minister of Great Britain, wisely stated, "Nurture your mind with great thoughts, for you will never go any higher than you think."21 The personality is made up of all a person's pre-earth and earthly thoughts (experiences)—so everything that a person thinks is important for personality development. The first step in changing a person's character is always to change his or her thoughts, and this happens when there are changes in their spirituality, desires, and values.

Thinking

Thinking is a sequence of symbolic processes that represent past learning and experience and shared meanings or understandings. People are symbol (words, objects) users, who engage in thinking throughout everything they do. Thinking is a constant flow of activity organized around life events people continually encounter that require some definition for decision-making.

This mind activity is necessary in every social situation throughout the day. It is sometimes less deliberate and conscious as with a minimal problem and decision, and at other times, it becomes more deliberate and conscious as when people are faced with a major problem and decision that requires them to analyze carefully a situation and consider the consequences of what they might do. Every situation people come across is new to some extent, and requires some problem solving. Every situation also has objects people make into social objects around the goals they seek. Each situation involves perceiving themselves in the situation, requires some adjustment on their part, and takes some covert action, some self-indication, and some rehearsal of various lines of action.22

The process of human thought is shown in the representation "The Human Thought Process." It shows that the choices of most people are greatly influenced by their desires or values. These desires determine people's priorities or goals in life and motivates them to achieve the priorities through various means that are deemed socially and morally appropriate by the individual as well as by significant other people and society. Of course, prior to any social action being taken to achieve our goals in life we must think and decide on a course of action to follow. Once a social action is taken, it results in a consequence.

Figure 6.1 The Human Thought Process

Desires ⟶ Motives ⟶ Thoughts ⟶ Actions ⟶ Consequences

Human Growth and Development

The English philosopher John Locke (1632-1704) said, "Children are travelers newly arrived in a strange country of which they know nothing."23 The first major tasks for a person arriving in this world of mortality are to learn to operate the physical body and to communicate by learning language. Thus, one of the challenges of mortality is for the spirit to learn to control the body appropriately, and the other major challenge, is to learn to communicate feelings and needs.

As life progresses, people find themselves passing through a number of stages, phases, transitions, existences, or episodes. Another way to view life is as a series of beginnings, and through each, people are being socialized every minute by a multitude of social forces and experiences.

Everything a person thinks, everything a person does, and everything that is done to a person modifies that person. As Alfred Lord Tennyson (1809-1892), the English poet said, "I am a part of all that I have met."24 Walt Whitman (1819-1892), a poet, also wrote, "A child went forth each day and became what he saw."25 Many have said that the eye is the window to the mind. Each thought that passes through a person's mind changes them from that point onward, and forever, they will be different than they otherwise would have been. When people think positive thoughts, they develop positive minds, and when people think negative thoughts, they develop negative minds. Every thought people think, good or bad, modifies their lives and changes them, and as a result, they are never the same again. Everything people do throughout life, and usually these are the little things they do, tends to push them toward a particular destination.

Often these stages are social and biological in nature simultaneously with each of these stages taking a person from one state of existence to another. Each stage has a purpose and occurs in some time sequence. All cultures recognize stages through which individuals pass during their lifetimes, and every culture has standardized rituals marking each of these stage transitions that are called "rites of passage." The most widespread rites of passage are those marking the arrival of puberty, marriage, and death. In essence, an individual becomes a different person each time he or she gets a new title, position, rank, identity, or whatever it may be. They also get new obligations, rights, and privileges. For instance, the passing of youth is like death in the sense that it is something a person will never get back again, and as a result, the individual is now another kind of person and in another phase of life.

A few people have attempted to describe human development in what are called life-course theories. One of the most prominent among these attempts is that of the psychoanalyst Erik Erikson (1902-1994), who describes how all individuals pass through a series of eight developmental stages from infancy to old age.26 Other similar attempts have been made to explain the cognitive development of children, the moral development of people, the stages of development in adulthood, and so on.

Human growth and develpment throughout life is a process whereby a person learns through different life events, trials, or problems, experience by experience (the *Law of Social Growth*). Life tends to be a series of trials that stack up like stairs with each trial preparing a person for the next one and each bringing them knowledge or experience. People tend to learn precept upon precept or, in other words, they tend to advance or continue from one degree of truth to another, from one area to another, and from one task to another. Humankind's experience with learning verifies this principle. Each individual's life tends to be a carefully laid out plan of individual trials that gives a person experience and gradual growth. This process is shown in the figure "The Cycle of Human Growth and Development Through Time."

People begin this process with a life event, with a problem or with adversity of some kind that enters a person's life. As you will recall from reading chapter 3 on the social laws, the *Law of Opposition* states there is opposition in social life and people can expect to encounter life events that will involve trials and problems. All people can experience such things as good, virtue, success, appreciation for well-being, and happiness, as well as, bad, corruption, failure, sickness and pain, and sorrow. It has been said there are two certainties in life: death and taxes.27 The sociologists Gerhard Lenski, Patrick Nolan, and Jean Lenski suggest adding technological advance.28 Actually, there is still another certainty in life, and that is, problems or adversities. Every person will experience misfortune, suffering, sickness, or other adversities. Adversity is the universal experience of all humanity.

Figure 6.2   The Cycle of Human Growth and Development Through Time

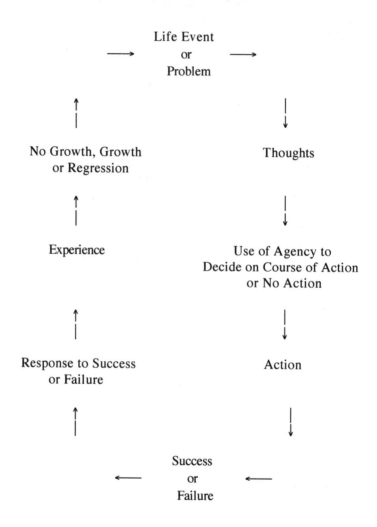

The poet Robert Browning Hamilton taught a lesson about pleasure and sorrow when he wrote in "Along the Road" that when he walked a mile with Pleasure she chattered all the way and he was no wiser after all she said. However, when he walked a mile with Sorrow she never said a word but he learned many things from her.29

As people encounter these life events or problems, they will think about how to deal with them in order to decide what they should do. This is suggested by the *Law of Action*. Much of this decision is going to be determined primarily by the person's values and desires that motivate them in life, as suggested by the *Law of Values*. However, we must also appreciate the power that social forces play in a person's everyday life. The process of making decisions in life involves sociohistorical factors that shape the type and number of alternatives open to a person. A person's knowledge of the range of alternatives open to them, various cultural and subcultural norms, a person's family background, economic and political forces, the person's age, race, class, gender, and religion, along with their personal values, will all affect the choices he or she makes. This is explained by the *Law of Motivations*.

As prescribed by the *Law of Agency*, people have the opportunity or agency to make choices in their response to these life events, except in those cases where some have taken over and impressed by force their own will and choice on the individual.

The choice a person eventually makes after thoughtful thinking, results in some course of social action, even including no action, which is a course of social action in and of itself. This follows from the *Law of Action*.

Every social action taken by a person is followed by a consequence (the *Law of Consequences*), which can generally be described as success or failure. What often may be more important than whether the social action leads to success or failure is the individual's response to this success or failure, because it is this response that develops the character of an individual over time. If successful, does the person remain humble or demonstrate arrogance. It is often in the depths of failure where persons learn the lessons that help them gain strength and develop strong and courageous characters.

Generally, a person may react in one of two ways to a failure by either becoming more kind and loving or becoming bitter. It is life events, and the responses to those life events, that gives each person experience and allows the person to grow and develop. In other words, it is only by overcoming problems and troubles and not submitting to them, that people can grow and build strength and character. As a result of a person's experience, they may not grow at all, they may even regress in their growth as a result of their response to a success or a failure, or they may grow in wisdom and in character.

What people become as individuals is a result of their values, motives, thoughts, and actions. The growth of a person is measured by what happens within himself or herself, or in other words, to the inner self or spirit and their spirituality. A knowledge of this spirituality reveals the progress of the human mind. It is spirituality that makes it possible to master human nature.

To illustrate further the cycle of human growth and development over time, lets examine an event encountered by many young people. Decisions facing today's young people are full of tremendous consequences. Many of them seem small at the time a person makes them, but the eventual outcome of these decisions can be almost overwhelming. For example, many young people meet with situations that offer them the chance to engage in sexual relations before marriage, and they are encouraged to do so by the new morality. Often this decision is made with little thought for its physical, mental, and spiritual ramifications, or is loss in the passion of the moment. Young people who decide to initiate sexual relations, with or without contraception, may result in nonmarital pregnancy. Unless there is a miscarriage, the young couple with a pregnancy must decide whether to marry, give birth to the child, abort the child, raise the child, abandon the child, or give it up for adoption. This, of course, assumes the young man will take partial responsibility for the pregnancy. If he does not, then the young women must decide whether to give birth to the child and become a single parent or have an abortion. If she gives birth to the child, she must decide whether or not to give the child up for adoption, or even abandon the child. She may even decide to commit suicide and kill herself as well as the child.

In the event she decides to give birth to the child, she must further decide how to support the child, including possibly marrying a newfound lover, or whether to remain at her parent's home, assuming this is acceptable to her parents, or to establish a new household. There are also implications for the child of a teenage mother, such as the survival of the child during the first year of life, the child's health problems, and the social and cognitive disadvantages of the child. In addition, there are consequences, such as marital dissolution for teen parents, emotional and psychological costs for grandparents, and the loss of contributions to the economy and the tax base for society.

Even when there is no conception of a child after engaging in premarital sexual relations, there can be other consequences of this action such as contacting a sexually transmitted disease (STD), of which, some like AIDS are deadly. Sexual freedom can result in venereal diseases as well as teenage pregnancies.

In this short illustration, the life event is a situation requiring a young person to decide whether or not they will engage in premarital sexual relations. The values held by those involved in this situation will have a large bearing on the outcome of their decision to actively engage in sexual relations. If they decide to engage in such activity, there can be a variety of consequences to this action for both people, ranging from behavior in the future to pregnancy and its related decisions, and actions on such things as giving life and support to a new child. Whatever action is taken, it results in a response and experience that influences the person's growth and development. It also demonstrates that much of the pain people can suffer, and inevitably impose upon others, is self-induced through their own choices. It further demonstrates how people's choices can even restrict their ability to exercise personal agency in the future.

Character

Years ago, the German philosopher Immanuel Kant (1724-1804) wrote:

> Intelligence, wit, judgement, and the other talents of the mind, however they may be named, or courage, resolution, perseverance, as qualities of temperament, are undoubtedly good and desirable in many respects; but these gifts of nature may also become extremely bad and mischievous if the will which is to make use of them, and which, therefore, constitutes what is called character, is not good.30

What is character? The character of an individual are the attributes or features that make up and distinguish the person. This is a person's total personality.

Anyone's character is developed through their daily lives and the test of human experience. Every choice made by a person leads to the development of his or her character. Crucially important in this process is a child's early years of life, which forms the foundation for his or her future. This has been demonstrated by various studies. There is evidence that certain attitudes are quite malleable and easily shaped even in late adolescence and early adulthood, but once they are formed they remain fairly stable throughout the remainder of the adult life span. This is supported by the findings of one of the most famous long-term studies in American sociology known as The

Bennington Study. This 50-year, three-stage, longitudinal study of the political development of a group of women, who were students at Bennington College in the 1930s and 1940s, showed that early adulthood provides fertile ground for the development of political attitudes that last a lifetime.[31]

A favorite saying is "We sow our thoughts, and we reap our actions; we sow our actions, and we reap our habits; we sow our habits, and we reap our characters; we sow our characters, and we reap our destiny."[32] In other words, it is a person's thoughts and behavior that shape their character and decide their destiny. It is a person's desires that direct the choices that shape his or her actions and make them what they are. In the end, an individual's character is the sum of all their thoughts. The greatest individual objective in life is to build character.

The character of a society is always the sum of its citizens' characters. As the political commentator George Will has argued, "one can judge a society by the character of the people it produces."[33]

Chapter 7

Social Relationships: The Connecting Links of Society

What is it that makes human society possible? Social relationships make human society possible. It is necessary for people to interact for society to begin, and it is only through further social interaction, that society can continue. There can be no society or community when there is no interaction.

Today, the fiber of American society, its social relationships, are coming apart. People are witnessing a general transformation of an American society from one that strengthens the bonds between people to one that is fraying the net of connections between them, as it moves toward individualism and a focus on the self and class rather than on the group and the whole.

Despite this development, all human beings are social in nature, and need others for survival. Each person depends on all others for their well-being. Individuals do not thrive in isolation, for they can only do that for a short time. This interaction is the process by which people act and react in relation to each other. Social interaction is vital to all people because it is through social interaction that every person grows and develops and sustains life. As the social psychologists Charles Horton Cooley (1864-1929) and George Herbert Mead and the psychologist Kenneth J. Gergen point out, it is a person's social relationships in groups that define them and create their sense of who they are.1 People are wholly interdependent upon others for their self development as stated in the *Law of Social Growth*.

While people are autonomous human beings with their own aptitudes and interests, they are at the same time, deeply dependent on others. This fact has been demonstrated in several cases of extreme childhood deprivation where children have failed to develop physically, mentally, emotionally, and socially, due to their lack of social interaction while in almost total social isolation. Studies have also demonstrated that love, affection, and attention are essential for a child's social and personality development, and that the lack of it, particularly in the early years of life, results in long-lasting emotional problems and personality defects.

It is also through social interaction that socialization occurs and people learn the culture of a society and become participants in society. It is during the process of socialization and interaction that social learning takes place and individuals share with others. They share not only their interests, concerns, needs, ideas, intentions, and feelings, but also the values, customs, facts, skills, and knowledge of a society that are passed on to the next generation. The social learning experienced by individuals influence their behavior throughout the remainder of their lives as well as the lives of all those with whom they come in contact (the *Law of Social Learning*).

To interact socially, people must share a language, culturally established meanings, and they must understand or have some notion of the identity of the person they are interacting with, and vice versa. As people interact, they exchange culturally established meanings through a wide variety of symbols, the most important of which is language. Language is the means by which people give meaning to feelings and ideas, and define their humanity to others. A person's communication is at the core of their relationships with other people and has consequences for those relationships.

Societies are made up of interacting individuals in social relationships. This means, people take into account each other when they act. In other words, one person acts with another in mind, and the other person acts with them in mind. So, what one person does at a point in time depends on what others are doing, and vice versa. Each person is acting and reacting to others. It is this social interaction that is the key to creating the reality that people perceive. The *Law of Social Interaction* tells us how a person acts is determined by their perception of social reality, which is based on the meanings of things in the world. These meanings of things are constantly modified through an interpretative process that individuals use in their dealings with each other, whereby, they interpret each other's actions as well as intentions. Therefore, people's perceptions of social reality develop through continued social interaction with other individuals and through a shared understanding about the meaning of behavior that involves putting themselves in someone else's shoes. A person's perception of social reality is important because it determines their behavior or actions.

As the Thomas theorem states, situations that are defined as real are real in their consequences. This also means that before a person can understand a situation, they must first arrive at an explanation of the way the situation was interpreted by the actors who are involved in the social interaction. Before a person can understand why a person behaves the way he or she does, they must first understand what he or she is thinking at the moment. Continued interaction that involves intentional communication and understanding facilitates not only cooperation, but also the resolving of disagreements, both of which are essential for the development and continuation of society.

People know how to act in a society based on rules of acceptable behavior. As infants are born into a society and are socialized through social interaction with others, particularly their families —the social group that has the primary responsibility for socializing new members in society—they learn what to do and what they should not do. They also learn how they should perform in various positions in a society, such as how to be a daughter or son, a father or mother, a student, a worker, a church member, and so on. Every one of these positions has culturally defined rights and obligations connected with them that inform individuals of behavior they can expect from others and others can expect from them. Essentially, the rights of one position correspond to the obligations of another position. The real essence of any social interaction lies in the rights and obligations of the members of society who fill its various positions. It is through this network of social relationships between individuals in various positions, who are constantly interacting and communicating, that societies develop and operate.

Social relations are power relations that may be equal or one-sided, and harmonious or antagonistic. Differences in power emerge when people have different resources. Since all people depend on one another, the inequality of resources leads to unequal dependencies. However, this does not necessarily mean that such unequal dependencies result in negative and destructive social relationships, although it can. In loving and respectful relationships, such as between children and parents where children are dependent on parents and parents have power over children, unequal dependencies are positive and constructive social relationships.

As people interact, a set of social patterns develops among them. These social patterns bring a certain stability to interaction. The overall pattern of social relationships is known among sociologists as "social structure." A social structure is a pattern of social relationships that forms the stable framework within which social interaction takes place. As people interact over time they establish relationships, and a set of positions arise. People fill these positions in relation to one another. Therefore, a position within this social structure makes sense only in relation to the other positions in the same structure. The position a person has is defined by his or her relationship to other persons within the social structure, which is expressed in behaviors toward them. Thus, it is by filling positions and acting in those positions that all of us contribute to society in a small but important way, and together all people accomplish whatever is necessary for a society. Even though people in their various positions may know of only a small part of the whole society, it is each person who is doing what has to be done for society to continue over time.

The structure of society builds up an interdependence among its citizens so that others become dependent on others in their positions, and they in turn, become dependent on them as they deal with them in their positions. This exchange of services and mutual dependence ties all people together. This interdependence gives recognition of the greater importance of our service to each other over our own individual self-interest. It is only through this recognition that our mutual services are going to continue. This interdependence further creates a commitment to society.

The most powerful emotion and force in the world is love. The vital importance of love for all humanity has been demonstrated and reiterated often in the study of near-death experiences. However, as significant as love is to people and society, scientifically we have only begun to research it. Nevertheless, unconditional love is the power of life, and it is absolutely crucial to all humanity. Vitally important for social life in a society, is the nature of its social relationships. When these social relationships are characterized by charitable interaction, it is conductive to peace within the society (the *Law of Charity*). This type of interaction is demonstrated by caring about other people, sharing with other people, giving to other people, sacrificing for other people, and even, serving other people. Love amongst a people is endeared through their service to each other. Obviously, people who are acting in kind, considerate, tolerant, helpful, caring, sharing, giving, respectful, charitable, and grateful ways in social relationships, greatly enhances the love feelings for people and commitment between people in social relationships. Love tends to beget love, just as hate begets hate. So, how a person acts tends to create the same behavior in those around them. As the *Law of Restoration* states, the social actions of people toward other people are restored to them. In other words, sooner or later our thoughts and actions come back to us in one form or another.

As individuals interact with each other they tend to form friendships with those who are in proximity to them and similar to them, particularly those who have similar values and stations in life (the *Law of Association*). This *Law of Association* unfortunately tends to divide society into various groupings, unless there is unconditional love and equality, and people have a greater commitment to the whole. As individualism increases to extremes, as is found in highly stratified or unequal societies, it is reflected in social relationships where people tend to interact only with those in similar positions. At some point, these highly stratified societies with their great divisions between the wealthy and the poor, show increasing strains and breakdowns in social relationships as opportunistic motives for social relations between people destroy the trust necessary for relationships (the *Law of Stratified Social Relations*).

Thus, it is social relationships that tie together the individual members of social communities to each other, and form the basis for the development and continuance of society as shown in "The Social Organization of Humanity" to follow. It is through these relationships that we discover ourselves. These social relationships are the very source of strength most likely to lift people up and give them the highest human fulfillment.2

Figure 7.1   The Social Organization of Humanity

Society

↑

-Which Constitute-

↑

Institutions

↑

-That Meets the Needs of Society Through Major Activities Known as-

↑

Social Relationships in Groups and Organizations

↑

-Results In-

↑

Individuals in Social Positions Socially Interacting

Chapter 8

The Family: The Keystone
of Society

A keystone is a stone that keeps an arch in place, and without it, the whole arch will collapse. This term is appropriate for describing the family, which is essentially the keystone of society. If families are strong, it strengthens the whole of society. President Abraham Lincoln (1809-1865) is reported to have said that the strength of a nation lies in the homes of its people. The family is society's most important group and institution, and has been throughout the history of humankind. The need for family is universal. It is the family that provides for intimate relationships and serves as the key link of the social chain of being.

Although there are other major social institutions in society, such as religious, educational, governmental, and political institutions, it is the familial institution that is the most important institution in the world. It is the very lifeblood of American society. Every known society has had the family. The family is the basic and universal institution (an institution is essentially a major human activity surrounding a basic need in society).

The family is, and has always been, the primary means of transmitting culture, including the transmission of moral and ethical principles, religious beliefs, attitudes about other people, and ways of understanding the world from one generation to the next. The family is basic because it has the vitally important task of socializing the new members of society—children. The family has by far the most influence in shaping children's destinies, and in forming their values, attitudes, and habits. It teaches children traditions and standards. Robert Nisbet stresses that individuals have the best chance of developing their talents and their identities as individuals within the context of family life.1 Psychologists and other experts state that a child's psychological development is determined almost entirely by parents in the family relationship. It is in the home, and with a family, that values are usually acquired and commitments to others are established. There are really no adequate substitutes for the family that have ever been found in the history of humankind, despite attempts to do so. The church, the school, and government programs can only reinforce and supplement what is acquired at home.

The Importance of Family

Why is the familial institution the most important institution? It is the most important institution because the survival of every society depends upon the continued existence and functioning of the family to ensure the replacement of members and to care, train, and develop the infant population. It is the institution where most of the problems of society can be cured.

The importance of the family has been demonstrated in several works. One of these works, was the monumental work, *The Decline and Fall of the Roman Empire* by the historian Edward Gibbon (1737-1794).2 In this work, Gibbon pointed out the vital importance of family, when he attributed the fall of that great civilization to:

1. The rapid increase of divorce and the undermining of the dignity and sanctity of the home, which is the basis of human society.

2. The decay of individual responsibility.

3. Higher and higher taxes and the spending of public monies for free bread and circuses for the populace.

4. The mad craze for pleasure; sports becoming every year more exciting and more brutal.

5. The building of gigantic armaments when the real enemy was within—the decadence of the people.

6. The decay of religion.3

Initially, Rome had strong families where the father was respected as the head of the family. In the early republic, the father had legal authority to discipline rebellious members of his family. The education of the children was the responsibility of the parents. This further strengthened the children's honor and respect for their parents, and contributed to the communication and understanding between parents and children. The strong Roman families produced a strong nation as evidenced by their victorious armies and prosperity. However, this changed over time.

The family of the ancient Romans is of special interest for understanding the family over time, because students of family have noted the similarities between the changes in the Roman family and changes in the family systems of modern Western civilization during the past century. In both instances, authority is weakened within the family, there is a movement toward equality of men and women, restrictive sex norms break down, and a historically rare condition emerges whereby either husband or wife can divorce the other at will. Some theorists have observed these changes occurred in the late stages of the Roman Civilization, and thus serve as indicators of the incipient decline and impending death of a civilization.4

A more recent experiment demonstrating the importance and necessity of the family, was "The Great Russian Family Experiment" studied by the sociologist Nicholas S. Timasheff. His study was a study of one of the most dramatic family experiments ever recorded. It was initiated in Soviet Russia between the two world wars by the Communists following the Russian Revolution in 1917. They believed that they had to abolish the family and other institutions associated with a capitalist system. They felt it was the nature of the family to preserve the traditions of a capitalist state, and therefore, the family had to go. In 1919, a soviet authority indicated that the family was no longer necessary in Russian society.

The goal was to destroy the traditional patriarchal family, where husbands were superior to wives and where parental authority was strong. Prior to the revolution, marriage was a religious institution and could only be put together or broken up by the church. One objective of the new regime was to liberate marriage from the bonds of religion. Therefore, church weddings were made illegal. All couples had to do was "register" their marriages with the government, and no ceremony about the significance of marriage was allowed. Beginning in 1917, divorce was made available simply for the asking. No reasons had to be given, and one's spouse could even be notified by postcard.

The antifamily campaign focused on other aspects of life too.

Incest and adultery were no longer criminal offenses. Abortion became legal in 1920. Inheritance rights ceased to exist. The distinction between legitimate and illegitimate children was dropped. Parental authority became weakened, and children no longer had to obey their parents if they did not follow strict Marxist teachings. Children could turn their parents in to government authorities. There were numerous family tragedies resulting from the state backing the children against parents.

In 1925 a new Family code was developed to help facilitate the destruction of the family. Now couples no longer had even to register their marriages. This in essence, led to the legalization of bigamy, a condition in which a man or woman could have many spouses. Promiscuity was common. At this same time, a new labor law made it a requirement that a person must accept any job assigned, and often husbands and wives were sent to live and work in different towns.

By 1930 the antifamily policies were largely successful—family ties were indeed significantly weakened. But there were a number of unforeseen problems, detrimental effects that were so strong that the very stability of the society was threatened. The birth rate dropped dramatically as a result of divorce and abortions. There were almost three times as many abortions as live births, and the divorce rate neared 40 percent. A nation on the verge of war with Germany saw its strength declining fast.

The whole society began to disintegrate; with the decreasing quality of parent-child ties, young hooligans roamed the streets. Juvenile delinquency, sadistic crimes, and gang wars and killings were not uncommon. In addition, the development of a "free love" philosophy and the "liberation" of women ended with females being exploited by Russian Don Juans. Millions of children were born without knowing parental homes.

The decline of the family became so costly that the Communist leadership reinstituted the family as the "pillar of society." The importance of marriage was emphasized again. Young people were encouraged to consider it as the most serious event in life. In 1939 an official Soviet journal made the amazing statement that the State cannot exist without the family. The journal also discouraged free love, and said that partners should see marriage as a lifelong union and encouraged them to have children.

Marriage was glorified again; marriage certificates began to be issued, and wedding rings became available once more. In 1936 divorce became difficult to obtain and also very expensive. Irrefutable evidence was needed. The concept of legitimate and illegitimate children reappeared. Mothers of illegitimate children no longer received state support. Abortion, once again, became a crime punishable with prison. Parents were given back authority over their children and were allowed to restrict their freedom. By 1944 marriages had to be registered, and they came to be the only legally recognized union.5

The Great Russian Family Experiment to get rid of the family had failed miserably.

These two works, and others, give historical evidence of the following:

1. The family is the basis of human society.
2. Society depends on the family for its continued existence.
3. Changes in a society, such as weakened family authority, equality of men and women, unrestricted sexual relations, marriage and divorce at will, and abortion, portend the breaking up of the family.
4. The breaking up of the family presages a collapse of a nation.

These particular studies also demonstrate that the destruction of the family is the cause of most social problems, and it can destroy a civilization, unless prompt action is taken to stop it.

The Industrial Revolution and the Family

In all societies, the preferred family pattern is one composed of at least a man and a woman joined in marriage with their biological or adopted children. However, in most of the world's societies, the most common family unit has been composed of a greater number of individuals known as the extended family. Throughout most of the history of humanity, people have also tended to live in patriarchal families and polygynous societies. As societies have become more industrial, their family patterns have changed.

In the 1940s, Carle C. Zimmerman, a family scholar at Harvard University, suggested a natural sequence of family forms occurred among the great civilizations.6 These family forms were: the Trustee Family System, the Domestic Family System, and the Atomistic Family System. He stated that early in the history of a civilization the family system was based on the supremacy of clans that provided structure, support, and protection for their members. The living clansmen saw themselves as holding family property and honor in trust from their ancestors with the responsibility to pass it on to future generations. This family form was the Trustee Family System.

The Domestic Family System comes with the emergence of centralized government that breaks up the clans into smaller family units. This system is typically father-dominated and emphasizes the importance of obedience and commitment. The most valued activities in this system are marriage and child rearing, and divorce is disapproved and rare.

Gradually, the Domestic Family System gives way to the Atomistic Family System that values personal rights and freedoms more than family loyalty and stability. According to Zimmerman, this individualistic family system curbs the father's power and greatly expands the rights and freedoms of women and children.

Zimmerman saw the trend in these family forms as leading to the fall of Greece and Rome before the irresistible power of tightly knit barbarian armies that were organized along clan lines. He felt that this happened because the atomistic families of the Greek and Roman Civilizations failed to instill discipline, loyalty, and obedience in their children.

Many sociologists trace major changes in the American family, and other family systems, to the Industrial Revolution and the consequent urbanization of society. They believe that industrializatioi was instrumental in transforming the authoritarian, large, and stable rural family system into a more equalitarian, relatively isolated, and unstable nuclear family.

They feel that with industrialization, work was removed from the home to the factories. The division of labor became more complex and the schools, not fathers, began teaching many occupational skills. They also saw that the use of these specialized occupational skills required young people to move away to the cities. Occupational success produced mobility upward in the social-class structure and further isolated parents and children from each other and their grandparents. Property became intangible, and ties to the land were lost. Thus, industrialization changes extended family systems into nuclear systems. Other general changes involved in the trend toward some variant of the nuclear family included: (1) free choice of spouse, (2) more equal status for women, (3) divorce and equal rights of divorce, (4) neolocal residence, (5) weakening of ties with extended kin, and (6) the pervasive philosophy of individualism that asserts the importance of the person over the group.

To provide some test of this argument, the sociologist William Goode assembled family data covering roughly the past 50 years in the West, Arabic Islam, sub-Saharan Africa, India, China, and Japan.7 He concluded that the alteration appears to be in the direction of some type of conjugal family pattern—that is toward fewer kinship ties with distant relatives and a greater emphasis on the nuclear family unit of couple and children. However, he found no simple cause-and-effect relationship between industrialization and the nuclear family, because nuclear families were found in primitive, non-industrialized societies as well as in modern ones.

Goode believes ideological changes (ideas about what most people in a society consider to be desirable—values) may be as instrumental for many of the changes in the family as the effects of industrialization. One such new ideology mentioned by Goode is that of "economic progress," the notion that technological development and the production of wealth is more important than the preservation of traditional customs. A second ideology he mentions is that of "individualism," the notion that personal welfare is more important than the family. A third ideology is "equalitarianism," a belief that women should have equal rights with men. Taken together, these emerging values may have been as instrumental in producing family change as the effects of industrialization, according to Goode.

Zimmerman's natural sequence of family forms within a civilization suggests various countries today display the Atomistic Family System. Goode's analysis further suggests that many of the characteristics of the Atomistic Family Form resulted not from the process of industrialization per se, but from a change in the values of the members of society.

In a postindustrial society such as the United States, the family appears to be completing the transition from a Domestic Family System to an Atomistic Family System. The family authority has been weakened as society has begun to place greater value on the individual than the group. Robert Nisbet has observed that one of Western Civilization's oldest and largest themes is what he calls "the decline of community."8 The English legal historian Sir Henry Maine (1822-1888) also observed the same theme when he stated in his Status-to-Contract thesis, that since ancient times the movement of progressive societies has been one distinguished by the gradual dissolution of family dependency and the growth of obligation to the individual in its place. He found in his research on ancient societies that the family originally predated the individual as the primary unit of society.9

Today in modern societies, the family has moved toward an egalitarian family pattern. Premarital and marital sex patterns have changed greatly. Family size has diminished, and divorce and remarriage rates remain high. Abortions continue to increase. For example, many of these changes can be traced to the 1960s and 1970s in America when there were dramatic changes in attitudes toward single status, marriage, premarital sexual activity, cohabitation, divorce, gender roles, childbearing, and abortion. Contemporary American families are now characterized by a diversity of family forms that include two-parent families, single-parent families, extended families, stepfamilies, binuclear families, gay and lesbian families, and cohabitating families. These families have arisen as a result of several trends, including a high divorce rate, an increasing rate of birth to single women, economic changes, and changing gender roles.

Socialization

Although the family has such major tasks to perform as reproduction, regulation of sexual activity, social placement of the individual in society, economic support of the family, and love and emotional support of the individual, its most important task is still to socialize new members of society. The family has always been the principle means of transmission of moral principles, religious beliefs, attitudes, world understanding, and habits of being from one generation to the next. In support of this observation, Arnold Green has persuasively argued that "the morality of the individual is ultimately dependent upon religious training in the traditional home."10

All sociologists recognize the importance of socialization on the kind of individuals that people become. Socialization teaches individuals their values, influences their actions, and helps form their central qualities. Socialization has a great impact on the choices people make, and the direction they will follow in their lives. Socialization through social interaction is the link between society and the individual.

The importance of socialization and its impact on a person is clearly demonstrated in the following two poems—one, a titled poem, and the other, an untitled poem—both written by knowledgeable and insightful unnamed authors.

CHILDREN LEARN WHAT THEY LIVE

If a child lives with criticism
He learns to condemn.

If a child lives with hostility
He learns to fight.

If a child lives with ridicule
He learns to be shy.

If a child lives with shame
He learns to feel guilty.

If a child lives with tolerance
He learns to be patient.

If a child lives with encouragement
He learns confidence.

If a child lives with praise
He learns to appreciate.

If a child lives with fairness
He learns justice.

If a child lives with security
He learns to have faith.

If a child lives with approval
He learns to like himself.

If a child lives with acceptance and friendship
He learns to find love in the world.

Anonymous

I took a piece of plastic clay and idly
fashioned it one day,
And as my fingers pressed it, still it
yielded and molded to my will.
I came again when days were past
The bits of clay were dried at last.
The form I gave it, it still bore, and I
could change that form no more.
I took a piece of living clay and gently
formed it day by day
And molded it with power and art—a
young child's soft and yielding heart.
I came again when days were gone.
He was a man I looked upon.
He still that early impress wore, and
I could fashion that form no more.

Anonymous

The philosopher and psychologist William James (1842-1910) also
notes that this socialization is a gradual and steady process consisting
of one act at a time:

Could the young but realize how soon they will become mere walking
bundles of habits, they would give more heed to their conduct while
in the plastic state. We are spinning our own fates, good or evil, and
never to be undone. Every smallest stroke of virtue or of vice leaves
its never so little scar. The drunken Rip Van Winkle, in Jefferson's
play, excuses himself every fresh dereliction by saying, 'It won't
count this time.' Well! he may not count it, and a kind Heaven many
not count it; but it is being counted nonetheless.... As we become
permanent drunkards by so many separate drinks, so we become
saints in the moral, and authorities and experts in the practical and
scientific spheres, by so many separate acts and hours of work.[11]

Today, many of the social problems in society are symptoms of the failure of the socialization process in the family. The place to cure most of the ills in a society begins in the homes of its members. The family is the chief source of a person's love, security, personal development, character formation, social welfare, education, prosperity, and happiness.

Even though most people think their most important job in life is their occupation, in actuality, the most important job any person will have is that of parenting because of the consequences it has for all society. There are no substitutes for good parenting. President Theodore Roosevelt (1858-1919) reaffirmed the importance of good parenting and home life when he spoke at the First International Congress on the Welfare of the Child in 1908:

> There are exceptional women, there are exceptional men, who have other tasks to perform in addition to, not in substitution for, the task of motherhood and fatherhood, the task of providing for the home and of keeping it. But it is the tasks connected with the home that are the fundamental tasks of humanity. After all, we can get along for the time being with an inferior quality of success in other lines, political or business, or of any kind; because if there are failings in such matters we can make them good in the next generation; but if the mother does not do her duty, there will either be no next generation, or a next generation that is worse than none at all.
>
> In other words, we cannot as a nation get along at all if we haven't the right kind of home life. Such a life is not only the supreme duty, but also the supreme reward of duty. Every rightly constituted woman or man, if she or he is worth her or his salt, must feel that there is no such ample reward to be found anywhere in life as the reward of children, the reward of a happy family life.12

The greatest influence on any human society is motherhood because of the major socializing responsibility that has been placed particularly on women. The home is the most important factor in the development of any child. It is the major responsibility of both parents to teach and train their children and to instill them with values that contribute to a good society. Value systems are built in the homes of a society, and they reflect those of parents. Thus, the values that people live by are to a large extent a function of the quality of their family life and the training they received when they were children.

The home is also the place where human character is best formed. Again, the most important element in a child's character development, and his or her subsequent attitude and conduct toward society, is the quality of the family life that he or she has had.

Every home can be seen as a school house of learning for good or bad. Although children come into the world with their own individual talents and strengths, they are still influenced in their growth and development by their parents. The best way to teach a child is by example. Children learn from parents to distinguish between right and wrong. When parents recognize the importance of their parenting role, and meet that responsibility, they help bring forth a better generation that contributes to a nation's growth and development. However, if they ignore their important role, families and nations are left in peril and often perish. Many of the problems that people have in their lives, and nations have, are due to the bad examples and teachings of their parents and forefathers.

Parental responsibility begins for both parents when the child is an infant, and is particularly important in the formative years from infancy to three years of age. The most effective families in socializing activities are characterized by love, and there is nothing that can replace it. Love, or caring, is the cornerstone of a strong family. Central to a strong family is the love a father has for his wife, and her love for him.

Families provide the basis for all intimate relationships in life. Those individuals who come from homes where parents place a strong emphasis on their own relationship and the strengthening of their bonds of love, display happy and secure marriages. This relationship between a husband and wife is the foundation upon which all other relationships in a family are built. The family environment established by the relationship between a father and a mother provides the example for a child as he or she interacts with others. The way a child feels he or she affects their parent's relationship is the single most important factor in a child's personality development and in the his or her attitudes toward future life. Studies show that stable environments and stable relationships with adults are crucial for a child's normal psychological development.

What people do with the family determines what will happen not only to the individual, but to the whole of society too. It is the spiritual strength of these families that determines the very well-being of society (the *Law of Family*). It also determines the well-being of the world, as Pope John Paul II states, "As the family goes, so goes the nation and so goes the whole world in which we live."13

Chapter 9

Society: The Sum of Its Membership

A society is made up of a self-sufficient group of people who live within common territory borders and share a culture and a language. This is the largest and most self-sufficient group in existence. Every society is the sum of its membership. In other words, societies become the sum of what their members do in their lives.

History shows that human populations have had a wide variety of societal types. Sociologist's have classified societies by a society's primary means of subsistence, on whether a society is preindustrial or industrial, on how members of a society relate to each other, on the complexity of the division of labor found in a society, on whether a society emphasizes secular concerns or sacred concerns, and so on. Another way to classify societies is to use the ideal categories of "spiritual societies" and "material societies." These societal types provide a more accurate description of societies as they are in reality and of their citizens real lives. They also encompass all the above mentioned classification schemes developed by sociologists and others.

Spiritual and Material Societies

A "spiritual society" is a society based on belief in the supernatural, sacred values, love, family, just social relationships, morality, and equality. People are valuable in this society. A "material society" is one based on belief in material things, secular values, disaffection, family decline, unjust social relationships, immorality, and inequality. Things are valuable in this society. Societies will have one set of characteristics or the other based on whether their citizens and leaders develop them, for a society has no mind of it own, only that of its membership.

Remember, these are ideal types of society that are useful for understanding societies. However, there is no society in existence that will match either of these ideal types perfectly, but only societies that are approximations of these types. In reality, there are societies in the world with varying degrees of the characteristics of the two ideal types of society. While some societies may be close approximations of a spiritual society, others may be close approximations of a material society, and still other societies, may lie on some point between these two.

Craig Lundahl recognized in the 1970s, as did Max Weber before him, and the sociologist Richard Johnson in the 1990s, that materialism and socioeconomic inequality are the root cause of both personal and societal conflict and destruction.1 The keys to identifying the onset and continuation of this destruction is the economy and the economic equality in a society. The market economy is nothing but the economic element of a free society and has no moral dimension of its own. However, it does represent the equality and morality of the people in the society. The social problems we observe in societies, such as crime, drug abuse, sexual deviance, and violence, are only symptoms or manifestations of the real problem—materialistic and economically unequal societies. This is because of the inextricable link between morality and economic equality (the *Law of Morality*). Other social scientists, particularly sociologists studying social stratification, are close to fully understanding these same principles, if they do not already.

The Social Order and the Development of Material Societies

How do these material societies develop? To answer this question, it is necessary to understand the moral and social order within societies, or the sequence of moral and social events that operate within societies. Thus, all societies have a social order that may best be understood by examining the "Causal Model of Social Order" on the following page.

Any examination of society begins with its individual citizens, because society is no more or less than the sum of what its members do in their lives. It is the members of society that create society's morality and social life. Therefore, a person's values and actions (the *Law of Values* and the *Law of Action*) not only have consequences for themselves, but also for future generations as people form families and transmit their values to their children. Of course, these individuals have been influenced by prior social and cultural characteristics in the society. As shown in the Causal Model of Social Order, it is individual values and actions that affect the moral and social fabric of the families in a society and are so crucial in the socialization of society's new members. The family is society's main way of transmitting to the next generation values and behavior. During the socialization process, the new members of society are taught the core values of society, and in that way, the parents of families, and their values, are instilled in the children of a society's next generation. The values and actions of parents and their children, and their children's children, help form the collective values and actions of society, since it is the values and actions of individuals in concert with one another that constitute the collective values and actions (the *Law of Collective Values* and the *Law of Collective Action*) of society. These collective values and actions have consequences for society and its well being (the *Law of Family*), just as personal values and actions have consequences for the individual.

It is this massive undertaking by the families of a society that provides the general goals to be sought in society, that is, what values are good and bad, right and wrong, and desirable and undesirable. In other words, the core values provide the broad guidelines for the social behavior in society.

These core values determine the direction of society. They also influence the direction as well as the moral and social fabric of other institutions. For example, the values and behaviors learned in the family directly affect the operation of the economy. In many societies throughout history, work has been something people did to survive. In these spiritual societies, such as in the early American colonial society, citizens stressed the simplicity of lifestyle, and any displays of wealth were scorned. Certainly, a society with such values develops an economy, a simple economy that provides the necessities of life, that is much different from one in which citizens are encouraged to own and consume goods and services and to accumulate

Figure 9.1   Causal Model of Social Order

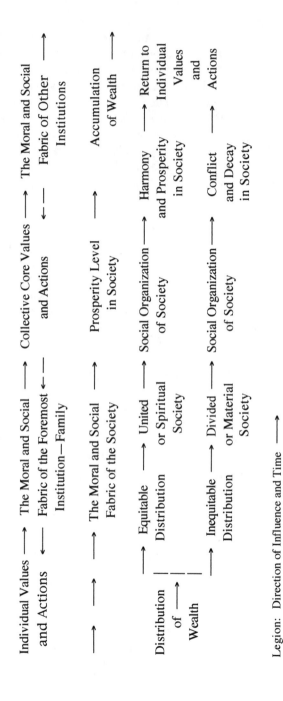

wealth or worldly goods, as symbols of the "good life," and of the owner's prestige.

The sociologist Talcott Parsons similarly theorized that what people in a society do, and a society does, is because of a common value system. He felt that the dominant value system in a society is shaped by the institution or institutions that a society gives primary importance to, which might be the family, the economy, or some other institution.2 Of course, today it is the capitalist economic system with its emphasis on the accumulation of private property and its profit minded orientation that is preeminent throughout most of the world. All countries seem to aspire to emulate this economic system that is found in capitalist societies.

The economy, in turn, affects the family as seen, for example, when there are low levels of economic activity (consumption) in a capitalist economy that result in unemployment and economic strain. These economic events are related to infant mortality, alcoholism, homicide, suicide, family abuse, family formation, separation, divorce, living arrangements, childbearing, marital satisfaction, marital tensions, family relations, and so on.

Another example of the direct affect of the family on an institution is education. The best predictor of performance in school is the quality of a child's family life. Strong families mean strong academic performance, and without a strong family, schools make little difference in learning because children learn most of what they know from a mother and father. It is their concern, involvement, strong support, and encouragement that is vital to learning. Despite national conferences on education, innovative teaching approaches, increasing expenditures on education, and educational reforms, America will not have strong schools until it solves the problems of its families. Material societies are particularly apt at using large sums of money in an attempt to solve social problems rather than understanding and dealing with their root causes.

The educational institution is an institution that should support and reinforce the socialization children receive within the family. In American society, for example, an approach called "decision making" was introduced in schools a few decades ago. Generally, it reflects the value structure found in the family and society as well as it influences the development of values. This approach replaced the earlier approach of character education, which encouraged students to practice habits of courage, justice, and self-control. Now, children are told to decide for themselves what is right and wrong (moral relativism), and they participate in so-called values-education programs that are little more than courses in self-esteem. These programs ignore the fact that self-esteem is mainly the result of strong families and parent-child interaction, not school courses.

In America, education is devoted to economic growth and increased productivity, and not moral values as it was once upon a time. This is true of all levels of education, including universities that are producing value-free teaching and research under the delusion they are being completely objective and that values have no place in rigorous scholarship. This shows a failure to understand the real nature of humanity where there are no neutral consequences, only good and bad consequences, or what some sociologists prefer to call functional and dysfunctional consequences. Educational values have certainly changed from the time of early universities where they were concerned with comprehending the universe to the 19th century American university where the most important course in the curriculum was moral philosophy, which was usually taught by the college president and required of all senior students, to the present time where universities teach students to get a job and make money. Allan Bloom has pointed out that contemporary education does not cultivate an understanding of or a love for the Western intellectual and religious tradition, which he says is the foundation of democracy and the cathedral of the soul. Bloom feels that American universities are not exposing student minds to eternal truths, but are leaving their students imprisoned in the culture of nihilistic relativism in which anything goes, as long as it goes fast and someone makes a profit.3 Thus, the moral decline of higher education in this century is representative of, and a part of, the cause for decline everywhere in society; in the elementary and secondary schools as well as in the family.

Just as the values taught in the family affect the economy and educational institutions, they also affect government and religion, and they in turn, affect the family. For example, as values taught in the family change they are reflected in the laws of government, such as the laws concerning divorce. At one time in the United States, it was difficult to obtain a divorce because it was thought to be in society's interest for people to stay together. Now, under the law, the individual interest is seen as more important than society's interest. If people want a divorce, they can obtain it. Of course, this also contributes to the destruction of the family institution.

The values taught by the family are reflected in the attempts by many religious organizations at restructuring and reforming themselves, and the development of new religious forms, ideologies, and structures. Some of these reforms and developments, such as changing roles of the church, modification of the central theological doctrines of faith, stances on social issues, and changes in the authority of the church, are done to conform to new value structures in society. These changes, in turn, tend to reinforce the values that are being taught by families.

Another example of core values and their affect on society and its institutions, is the human activity of health—another institution found in modern societies. The dramatic change in family structure in modern societies is having a powerful impact on health. The consequences from the changing family structure is being felt in all aspects of society, but particularly in the health and well-being of children. In America, for example, a child raised in a single parent household has a health disadvantage regardless of whether the child comes from the rich, middle, or poor class. Fatherless homes and non-intact family settings are related to various youth problems that include psychiatric problems, suicide, poor educational performance, violent behavior, use of drugs, lack of self-control, gang membership, and crime. America also experiences a high rate of infant mortality and female and child poverty because of single parenthood and illegitimacy. Despite the government's attempt to deal with the problems of poverty and health among these affected families, it can never substitute for a good family. Government will continue to have limited success until values change and families are strengthened.

The interaction, in many ways, between the various institutions of society results in institutions being the cause (the family being the major cause and other institutions secondary causes), and at other times, being the effect of social patterns in the larger social structure of society. Thus, all institutions are interrelated with the larger society in a multifaceted and complex manner based on collective values. It is these values, initially learned in the family, that permeate throughout society and determine its moral and social fabric, and reverberates back again to the very core of society, the individual.

To this point, it has been assumed that a spiritual society exists with its emphasis on the supernatural, sacred values, love, family, just social relationships, morality, and equality. These values and societal characteristics are associated with the prosperity level in a society.

The people of a society who display charity, compassion, love, gentleness, humility, kindness, mercy, meekness, patience, selflessness, and submissiveness become prosperous. All societies have material and non-material resources such as food and honor to allocate to its citizens. It is through the labor of society's citizens that the material resources are produced, as stated in the *Law of Work*. As people contribute to production in society by cooperating and helping each other with respect and love, society accumulates resources— referred to as the accumulation of wealth.

Societies determine how to distribute their resources or accumulated wealth. As shown in the Causal Model of Social Order, this distribution of resources can be done equitably among the members of society, or it can be done inequitably. If the distribution is done equitably among the members of society, the society is in compliance with the *Law of Shared Resources*. This results (the *Law of Compliance and Collective Consequence*) in a united or spiritual society where people are the same with the only differences between them being what sociologists call "social differentiation." Social differentiation is a condition where people have distinct individual qualities and roles to play. For example, people are differentiated by biological characteristics, such as sex, size, strength, and agility, and by social roles such as mother, father, son, and daughter, and work tasks or occupations. These differences in biological characteristics and social roles are just that—differences. These differences do not designate that one personal quality or one work role is more important than another, or that the person who possesses the quality or fills a work role is better than another person with a different quality or who fills a different work role. United or spiritual societies are moral societies that believe in a supernatural power greater than themselves, follow values passed from one generation to the next through strong religious traditions, love and value all members of society, cherish families and the raising of children, believe in and practice fair and honest relationships between their members, and believe all people should share in society's resources.

These values and characteristics of a united society influence the social organization of society. The social organization of every society is made up of the patterned social relationships among individuals and groups that were discussed in chapter 7. As suggested earlier, these relations of a united or spiritual society are fair, honest, positive, productive, and filled with charity. Such a society is filled with harmony and happiness among its membership, and it continues to experience prosperity. The members of this society display humility. These behaviors perpetuate similar values and actions in all members of the society.

If the distribution of resources is done inequitably among the members of society, then the society fails to comply with the *Law of Shared Resources*. This occurs when the values in a society change and its priorities become fixed on the acquisition, use, or possession of things or wealth (the *Law of Materialism*). Once the members of a society value materialistic pursuits and material well-being, they begin to compete for wealth, power, and prestige (the *Law of Collective Action*); the three factors contributing to inequality identified by Max Weber.4 This will eventually result in a divided or material society (the *Law of Division*) where people are treated differently and there is unequal resources between them. This is what sociologists call "social inequality." Social inequality is a condition where people have unequal access to valued resources, services, and positions in society. Individual characteristics and different social roles and positions may be valued unequally or ranked from superior to inferior. For example, in societies where physical strength is important in providing the necessities of life, the strong may be able to successfully demand greater rewards and, consequently, greater respect. In modern societies, with their large and diverse labor forces or divisions of labor, it is those in positions of coordinating and organizing the work of others who obtain more authority. This is pointed out in the theoretical work of the sociologists Ralf Dahrendorf and Gerhard Lenski.5 Such authority is usually used to acquire greater resources.

These differences in authority or power designate that one personal quality or one work role is more important than another, and that the person who possesses a more important quality or fills a more important work role is better than another person with a lesser quality or a lesser work role.

Divided or material societies are immoral societies seeking leisure and physical and sexual pleasure, are heavily steeped in conflict (the *Law of Inequality*), believe in their own power and worship worldly things such as money and famous people, have members who are obsessed in seeking after worldly success and religious and professional positions, follow the process of reasoning and man-made values, love and value society's wealthy members, give importance to individuals rather than groups such as families, believe in and practice selfish, unfair, and dishonest relationships between their members, and believe some people should have a greater share of society's resources.

These values and characteristics of a divided society influence its social organization. The relations between society's members tend to be dishonest and distrustful, and their ultimate purpose is personal gain (the *Law of Stratified Social Relations*). Such a divided society is filled with conflict (as suggested by the social theorists Karl Marx and Ralf Dahrendorf) and unhappiness among its membership, and it continues to experience failure and decline. The members of this society display selfishness and the pride in their title, income, dress and appearance, and place and station in society. This society perpetuates similar values and actions in its members. If the collective values of a divided society do not change over time, the society will eventually destroy itself or weaken itself to such an extent that external enemies will destroy it. In essence, people in any society get the life they deserve whether it be good or bad.

A society operates not only within its own social environment, but also within biophysical and global (society) environments. A spiritual society will tend to care for and live in harmony with the biophysical environment and preserve it, while a material society will tend to exploit it in their strivings for materialistic pursuits and profits. The social and biophysical environments are interdependent and can affect each other dramatically. However, an examination of this and the global relationship is beyond the scope of this book.

Middletown: An Example of the Development from a United Society to a Divided Society

A classic sociological study that clearly illustrates the social processes involved in the transition from a united or spiritual society to a divided or material society was done by the husband and wife team of Robert S. Lynd (1892-1970) and Helen Merrell Lynd in the 1920s and 1930s in Middletown (Muncie, Indiana). The study began when the Lynds went to Indiana to describe a "typical" American community as it existed in 1924. Then, Middletown had 35,000 inhabitants. To have a baseline for contrast, the Lynds reconstructed life in 1890 when the town had only 11,000 people and was going through the first stages of industrialization. They eventually returned to the city in 1935 and wrote of its growth to 47,000. Thus, they had three points of time to contrast: 1890, 1924, and 1935.

The Lynds lived in the town for over a year, meeting and talking to as many people as possible. They interviewed all the important people, and many of the unimportant ones too. They read newspapers, diaries, and local histories. They went to various ritual gatherings of church and civic groups and luncheon clubs. Occasionally, they passed out questionnaires to get standardized information about such matters as budget behavior or attitudes of students in the high school.

As the Lynds' study progressed, they wrote that it became increasingly apparent that the money medium of exchange, and the cluster of activities associated with its acquisition, drastically conditioned the other activities of the people. The Lynds observed two kinds of activities in the workday life of the community in 1924. The people who engage in them are the working class and the business class. They observed that members of the first group largely address their activities in getting their living primarily to things, using material tools in the making of things and the performance of services. Members of the second group, the business class, address their activities predominantly to people in the selling or promotion of things, services, and ideas. There were two and one-half times as many people in the working class as in the business class (71 out of every 100 people).

They also found that being born upon one or the other side of the watershed roughly formed by these two groups was the most significant single cultural factor tending to influence what a person does all day long throughout their life; whom the person marries; when they get up in the morning; whether they belong to the Catholic or Presbyterian Church; if they drive a Ford or Buick; whether or not their daughter makes the desirable high school club; if their wife meets with one club or another club; and so on indefinitely throughout the daily comings and goings of a Middletown's men, women, and children.

One of the central themes of the first Middletown volume published by the Lynds was that, from 1890 to 1924, there were basic changes in the work pattern of both the business and the working classes—changes that resulted in a wider gap between them. These changes flowed from three causes according to the Lynds: a larger population, more machinery, and, most importantly, an increasing emphasis on money.

The Lynds described in vivid detail a case study of the great transformation of modern life—industrial capitalism. Middletown in 1890 was a market town that was just beginning to turn to manufacturing. The work habits and values of its people were extensions of the traditions of their farmer parents. Those farmers were people who had conquered a wilderness when there had been land for all who would work it. The land provided plenty for everyone. This was a society that lacked gradations of rank and privilege. It was a society that stressed individual initiative and progress, family solidarity, simplicity of manners and style of life, and equality among neighbors.

As manufacturing succeeded farming, the base of livelihood developed a gradation in income that extended from unskilled through skilled laborers to bosses and a few professional men. Initially, the gradation was not sharply divided into levels and a man often moved through several steps in a few years. It was understood that the system was open to everybody in fair and equal competition.

By 1924, Middletown was becoming too large and its productive system too complex and mechanized for community prestige to flow automatically from skill at work. People did not understand the nature of the activities of others. Concurrently, money was becoming increasingly important as more spheres of life became parts of the commercial market. The result was people began to use money as a sign of accomplishment, a common denominator for prestige. The question "How much does he earn?" was heard more frequently than "How much skill does he have?"

When the Lynds returned to Middletown in 1935, they found Middletown had grown larger and its industrial plant more mechanized and more subservient to national corporations. Middletown had gone through the boom of the late 1920s and the devastating crash of the early 1930s. It was now a more divided community with a new class structure consisting of six different classes.

In a period of approximately 50 years, Middletown had gone from a community similar to a spiritual or united community that followed the traditions of their farmer parents with equality and no divisions between themselves, stressing family solidarity and simplicity of manners and style of life, to a material or divided community based on the importance of money and prestige where greater shares of society's resources were given to those members who supposedly were engaged in more important work than the work of others.6

Change in the Social Structure of Society

As the *Law of Social Change* states, it is the spiritual or material pursuits of the members of society that change the entire social structure of society, which includes every social institution in society. This is represented on the following page in the "Model of

Change in Social Structure."

As shown in the Model, all aspects of society are affected by its level of spirituality (the *Law of Collective Spirituality*) as expressed through the collective values of its citizens (the *Law of Collective Values*). Anytime the level of spirituality in a society increases so does its morality. This change results in the strengthening of the family that influences the success of the nation's educational system. The level of spirituality and humility is related to the amount of equality and prosperity a society will experience, and they increase as the level of spirituality increases. At the same time, the size and power of government decrease and people are given more liberty or freedom.

However, once a society begins to pursue materialistic values, this entire dynamic relationship will begin to change as represented in the Model. This kind of value change can happen within as short a period of time as a generation or 25 to 30 years, or in a slower period of time such as 300 years or more. When the value change does happen, the opposite of spirituality—materialism and pride—begins to dominate society. First, the level of morality in a society declines. According to the *Law of Morality,* the more materialism and inequality in a society, the more immorality, dishonesty, and selfishness that will be experienced in it. So, as morality declines in society, all kinds of immoral behavior such as selfishness, dishonesty, crime, corruption, immoral lifestyles, violence, and so on, can be expected to occur. Dishonesty, of course, fosters mistrust that is so important for social relationships between people as well as it undermines charity and destroys the unity in a society.

This value change is also accompanied by a decline in family strength and in the success of the educational system. The level of materialism is also related to the amount of inequality and prosperity a society will experience, with inequality increasing and productivity declining, as shown in the Model when the level of materialism increases.

Once a belief in certain absolute truths, such as the existence of a higher power and the reality of immortality are lessened or loss (scared values), there is a sharp gain in the size and power of governments, and people have less liberty. This is also true for democractic governments that require a moral and religious or spiritual people for effective operation. These governments, with extremely inequitable distributions of income, experience a breakdown of democracy.[7] In turn, the rise of democracy and liberty is linked to a

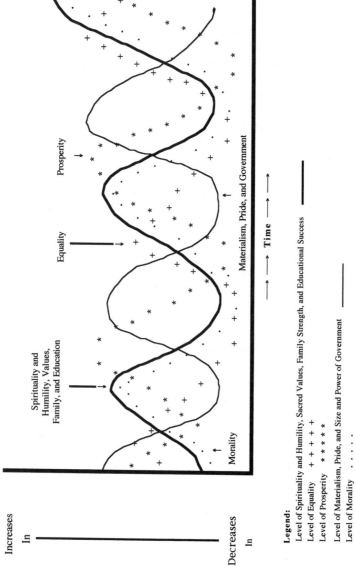

Figure 9.2   Model of Change in Social Structure

thriving economy and, most importantly, equitable distribution of incomes and resources. The survival of these free and open societies are dependent upon spiritual values, equitable distribution of income, and moral conduct. The state never withers away in a standardless (moral relativism) society, but rather it swells and becomes more strong, particularly the central government.

The Cycle of Humanity

Various historians, such as Edward Gibbon, Oswald Spengler (1856-1936), Arnold Toynbee (1889-1975), and Will Durant have analyzed the reasons for the fall of civilizations. They have suggested history is a pattern of growth, breakdown, and decline, although Durant is less sure of what the results will be for the developed and complex civilizations of today.8

The views of sociologists in this century seem to diverge widely on this issue. One sociologist, Pitirim A. Sorokin (1889-1968), suggests humanity goes through a wave-fluctuation between two major culture styles, the "ideational" and "sensate" cultures, which Sorokin and his associates traced back to the days of ancient Greece. They said an ideational culture is based on truth revealed by the grace of God through his prophets or oracles and a sensate culture is based on truth derived only through the sense organs (science). In other words, there are two basic types of societies, those that emphasize things that can be thought about but not necessarily felt through the senses and those that emphasize things that can be sensed.

Sorokin saw modern societies as characterized by sensate values, and even made several predictions about what would happen if America were to continue its development of sensate values. They were as follows:

1. Senate culture will increasingly lose its sense of distinction between right and wrong, beautiful and ugly, and the more abstract human values because of its materialism and objectivity.

2. People will increasingly be interpreted in mechanical and material terms and the spiritual basis of human worth would be lost.

3. With universal values lost, there will be a loss of binding and pervasive consensus and dissensus will dominate.

4. Contracts and covenants will lose the remnants of their binding power and the contractual socioculture house built over preceding centuries will collapse.

5. Force and fraud will be required to maintain moral order.

6. Freedom will be constrained and used as a myth of control by an unbridled and dominant majority.

7. Government will become more unstable and more inclined to resort to violence.

8. The family will continue to disintegrate because of the decline of universal values and the intrusion of sensate values.

9. The sensate culture will tend to become shapeless as undigested but sensually appealing cultural elements are dumped onto the environment.

10. "Colossalism"—what's biggest is best—will replace the values given to quality. Those with "gimmicks" will be valued over those with genus, and the creativity of the system will wane. Because valuable things are not, by any means, necessarily negotiable in our society, what is negotiable will win out.

11. Anarchy will increase and creativity decrease, depressions will grow worse, and levels of living will deteriorate.

12. Security of life will diminish and suicide, mental illness and crime will increase.

13. The populace will divide into two parts. On one hand, will be the sensate valued "hedonists" who seek indulgence and pleasure. On the other hand, will be those who withdraw and become antagonistic to these values (Ideationalists).9

Spengler, Toynbee, and Sorokin distill from their comparative studies of history the attributes of decline to the West, including America, in the present time.10

Generally, sociologists tend to see civilization as a cumulative process that is interrupted by setbacks and human catastrophes and is modified in its course by culture contact and diffusion.

More recently, Robert Nisbet sees the undermining of the America resulting from a decline of a belief in progress. He suggests that such a weakening in this belief has resulted from the erosion of five fundamental assumptions that made Western societies great: a belief in the value of the past, a conviction that Western civilization is superior, a faith in reason, an acceptance of the worth of economic and technological growth, and a belief in the worth of life on earth. Nisbet says the disenchantment with progress that occurred with the affluence the nation experienced after World War II led to impatience and restlessness, and then eventually to boredom. This decline in the belief in progress is also associated with a similar decline in the family system. He says that the hedonism, narcissism, and rampant sexuality in the United States today is a result of boredom. In essence, Nisbet is suggesting a weakening of beliefs as a result of affluence leads a nation through a series of stages to a gloomy future where the social bonds that hold the society together will break. Then, says Nisbet, unless America returns to a belief in progress, it will become the first democratic totalitarianism, a bureaucratic despotism, and it will be followed by a final collapse of anything resembling a free society.11

The historian Christopher Lasch sees progress as pure myth, simply a dream that is not supported by history. He states that the modern idea of progress is one in which society's advancement is equated with increasing consumption. To escape this consumption mentality, Lasch sees society following the "the prophetic" tradition of the theologians Jonathan Edwards and Reinhold Niebuhr and the philosophers Ralph Waldo Emerson and William James. This tradition tends to emphasize responsibility rather than freedom and limits rather than choices. Lasch sees human existence as one characterized by tragedy and struggle rather than by endless growth.12

The Greek philosopher Plato (427?-347 B.C.) reduced political evolution to a sequence of monarchy, aristocracy, democracy, and dictatorship.13

The historian Arthur M. Schlesinger Jr. in his collection of essays, *The Cycles of American History*, alludes to a cyclical pattern of events in American political history today. Schlesinger feels that American politics runs in 30-year cycles of desire for public action that are followed by periods of disenchantment, private interest, boredom with materialism, and then a return to public purpose and the beginning of another cycle. He suggests that the shifts in cycles move in tandem with generational changes, and that there was another marked change in the direction of American life around 1990. Schlesinger believes the United States is beginning to move into a time when public action will be dominant again.14

The historians William Strauss and Neil Howe see modern history as a cycle of four turnings with each cycle spanning roughly 80 to 100 years or a long human lifetime. They see the aging of generations or generational forces underlying the turnings of history called growth, maturation, disorder, and destruction. A rebirth follows, and the cycle starts over. America is in the third turning, or disorder.15

Frank J. Sulloway suggests that social change may "be due in part to the varying proportions of first borns in different eras."16

It has also been observed by several other observers that societies and civilizations pass through a cycle of righteousness, in which they rise from oppression to liberty and abundance, only to succumb through selfishness and corruption to governmental dependence, and finally, to destruction. For example, in 1671, the English poet John Milton (1608-1674) wrote that nations who become corrupt are brought to servitude by their vices and love bondage with its ease more than they do liberty because it is too strenuous.17

Edward Gibbon wrote of the collapse of Athens by saying:

> In the end, more than they wanted freedom, they wanted security and they wanted a comfortable life. And they lost it all—security, comfort, and freedom. The Athenians finally wanted not to give to society, but for society to give to them. When the freedom they wished for most was freedom from responsibility, then Athens ceased to be free.18

John D. Lawrence traced the rise and fall of nations to the following eight steps:

> From bondage to spiritual faith.
> From spiritual faith to courage.
> From courage to freedom.
> From freedom to abundance.
> From abundance to selfishness.
> From selfishness to complacency.
> From complacency to apathy.
> From apathy back again to bondage.19

It has been suggested that the United States today is somewhere between selfishness and complacency, or maybe a little beyond complacency.

Certainly these views of the evolution of societies and civilizations have merit, but those with more creditability are those that see cyclical patterns in societies and civilizations, some of which, are very similar to the true nature of this process in the world.

Throughout the history of humankind, civilizations and societies have tended generally to follow a cyclical pattern of development, with civilizations and societies relearning the same lessons that those who preceded them learned. "The Model of the Cycle of Humanity," shown on the following page, describes this cycle of stages that societies and civilizations follow in their development as they move from a spiritual to a material society, and back to a spiritual society.

The cycle begins with a society that has the characteristics of equality and morality that causes prosperity and happiness, and wealth for all its citizens—all characteristics of a spiritual society. Of course, reference to the characteristics of equality and morality means that resources in the society are distributed equitably or nearly equally among society's citizens. They also have strong and traditional religious or scared values they follow—they are what some would describe as "righteous." These resources (wealth) are abundant because of the citizen's labor, cooperation, industriousness, and productivity. Such a society is a successful, flourishing, and thriving society that experiences healthy economic growth, economic well-being, and great prosperity.

However, the accumulation of wealth can have, and often has, a disastrous effect in any society, and the most disastrous effect it can have is the inequality it causes. People's attitudes and values toward wealth can begin to change because they have a propensity for material goods and are unable to resist the appeal of wealth and the things and pleasure it can buy. The desire for money begins to overwhelm every other human consideration. Now, the economic factor that so dominated Karl Marx's writings, becomes of primary importance.20 Great wealth also brings with it security, power, and position. It also brings an easy life. In time, members of society, particularly ambitious men and women, may begin striving and competing for wealth. Inequality is not only the result of wealth seeking, but may actually be its purpose sometimes so that some people can have more resources, power, and prestige than other people. President Abraham Lincoln experienced firsthand the interplay of ambition, power, and glory. He wrote:

Figure 9.3   Model of the Cycle of Humanity

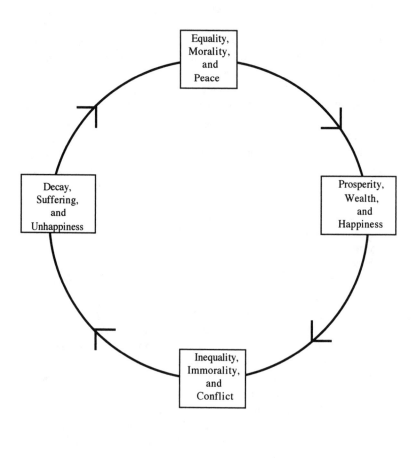

← ← Time ← ←

This field of glory is harvested, and the crop is already appropriated. But new reapers will arise, and they, too, will seek a field. It is to deny, what the history of the world tells us is true, to suppose that men of ambition and talents will not continue to spring up amongst us.... Towering genius disdains a beaten path. It seeks regions hitherto unexplored. It sees no distinction in adding story to story, upon the monuments of fame, erected to the memory of others. It denies that it is glory enough to serve under any chief. It scorns to tread in the footsteps of any predecessor, however illustrious. It thirsts and burns for distinction; and, if possible, it will have it, whether at the expense of emancipating slaves, or enslaving freemen.21

Once citizens begin seeking wealth they become very proud, which engenders contention and conflict, and they start feeling they are better than others. They begin to divide into classes based on wealth and levels of learning with each having their own class-based interests. Some classes dominate others as they now are competing with each other for wealth as well as power and prestige. This is the very conflict between classes that is mentioned by Marx, Dahrendorf, and other theorists. The more important wealth becomes, the less important it is how a person gets it. Ethics begin to disappear. In other words, throughout history, immorality has always been associated with the pride of wealth.

It is the moral fiber of society that is the key to society's eventual decline and fall; for the moral strength of any society, is the sum of the moral strength of its citizens. Evidence of this begins to appear everywhere. For example, it can be seen in the government and the laws of a society as those persons guilty of crimes go unpunished because of their money. People even begin to form secretive organizations for the sole purpose of gaining wealth and power, including controlling the government, such as seen in the recent example of the South American country of Colombia. These organizations may pursue this course to the point of even destroying government and society. They tend to thrive in affluent societies, and fade during times of poverty. These organizations will eventually destroy a society unless a society destroys them first, because they require a complacent society to host and support them. Once inequality exists in a society it is perpetuated, and where people are located in the class system is perpetuated, so that the net effect over time is even greater inequalities.

An unequal society experiences decay, suffering, and unhappiness that result from the fierce competition by people to improve their rank (such as those who are the near rich or upper-middle class), and by the rich to stay rich as they work within carefully created structures to protect their wealth (such as prep schools and prestigious universities, exclusive clubs, resort communities, and remote residential areas) or to get richer. Most of the social problems in a society are caused by social inequality. An unequal society, in large part, is the cause of poverty, crime, miserable work, exploitation of other people, lack of self-worth, stress, institutions that produce and maintain suffering and unhappiness, and destructive conflict. These consequences of inequality are associated with the lack of productive work, unemployment, poor physical and mental health, family stress and disorganization, lack of educational opportunity, inadequate protection under the law, drug abuse, alcohol abuse, prostitution, selling illegal drugs, violent crimes, gangs, price fixing, property crimes, lack of civility, respect, and kindness, abused wives and children, fear, anger, mental illness, suicide, violence, wars, corruption, political extremism, distrust, famine, homelessness, sexual immorality, and other social problems. Inequality brings suffering to large segments of the population, and that suffering, in turn, will eventually bring misery to the rich and powerful along with the poor. This will threaten the continuation of society's social institutions, and society itself. This humbles proud people and reduces their differences as hardships of many kinds bring them closer together with the poor. They tend to return to religion and sacred values causing a renewal of society, as suggested by Duke and Johnson's research findings in chapter 4.

Society never improves of itself. A society reacts only to the actions of those who live in it. The transformation of a society always begins with its citizens. The people of a society can quickly change as history has demonstrated and slow down or speed up this cycle. Recent history shows how millions of Germans and Italians, individually and collectively, changed completely from one state of mind to another, or from one value structure to another, in a matter of a few short years. The downfall of the Soviet Union is yet another dramatic example of how ideas changed one value structure to another in a very short time. There is always the possibility of the Cycle of Humanity stopping at prosperity and wealth, depending on society's value structure and the distribution of wealth, or at decay and suffering until the eventual extinction of society.

The Greatest Threat to Society

What is the greatest threat to a society? It is material prosperity and the life of ease it engenders. The prologue to disaster in society is always the accumulation of wealth. Wealth can be a blessing or a curse, depending on a people's attitude toward it, and their use of it. Most of humanity cannot resist the appeal of wealth and the things it can buy. They begin to strive for wealth and what wealth brings—prestige and power. This leads to the most disastrous effect of the accumulation of wealth—inequality in society. Also, as Robert Bork states, "affluence brings with it boredom, of itself, it offers little but the ability to consume, and a life centered on consumption will appear, and be, devoid of meaning."22 This is soon followed by immorality and members of society seeing themselves as better than others, and dividing into classes. The division of society into classes, and the accumulation of wealth in the hands of comparatively few individuals and powerful organizations, is the sure precursor of a society's ruin.

Chapter 10

The Good Society

What constitutes the best society has been described from philosophers, such as Plato, to Utopians, such as the English statesman and author Sir Thomas More (1478-1535). A more recent effort at describing a good society began with the work of Graham Wallas (1858-1932), who published a book in 1915 entitled, *The Great Society*. He influenced the philosopher John Dewey (1859-1952) and the journalist and philosopher Walter Lippmann (1889-1974), whom both wrote about the same subject. Dewey looked toward a "Great Community" that would be a new society based on the enlargement and enhancement of democracy throughout society's institutional structures. Lippmann foresaw an interdependent and technologically abundant global society that would allow for the possibility of a global order of security based on equity, which would be in the interests of everybody.

In 1992, the sociologist Robert N. Bellah and his associates published a book entitled, *The Good Society*; a book that draws on the work of Dewey and Lippmann, as well as, a number of other observers and analysts of the modern world. Bellah and his associates state "that there is no pattern of a good society that we or anyone else can simply discern and then expect people to conform to."[1] Unfortunately, Bellah and his associates begin their impressive work on a false premise. In fact, there is a pattern for a good society that can be discerned, and there is but one path that leads to it. In order for any society to be a good society its membership must conform to this pattern or closely approximate it.

Earlier, we generally described the spiritual society as a society based on a belief in the supernatural, sacred values, love, family, just social relationships, morality, and equality. How does such a spiritual society operate? This is a society where people believe in a higher power and sacred or religious values, and will voluntarily accept and abide by those values. This is essential for a spiritual society because it is only when the members of such a society reach a high level of spirituality that a good society can evolve and thrive. This is a society where the quality of life of the whole is more important than for the individual. It is a society where the quality of life for all is raised through power sharing and joint ownership of the economic, educational, and governmental systems. It is a society where each member's talents are used for the common good and all things are held in common among society's members so that none are rich and none are poor, but all share in earthly things. It is a society where each person has a position and employment, and where there is no idleness. All persons labor or work according to their ability and keep only those resources they justly need. This way every person who has needs may be amply supplied and have the resources they need. Surplus resources are utilized for the common wealth and for the less fortunate or poor and sick members of society according to their just need. Thus, none are in debt, but all are free and equal in the sense that society's resources are distributed according to the needs of each family or person, allowing all members of society the opportunity to enjoy society's resources, which they should. Every person deals justly and cooperates with one another in transactions of mutual benefit. There is no contention, no envy, no immorality, no crime, and no class structure among the population, because they are as one and filled with charity for one another.

The characteristics of the spiritual or good society are:

- A sincere high level of spiritual awareness among all members of society
- Members of society love their neighbors as they love themselves
- The interest of the whole group is uppermost in the mind of each member of society
- All members of society are equal with each member enjoying equal rights and privileges
- A sharing society

- All distribution of society's resources are on the basis of just need and labor with each member of society having ownership in the economic system
- Members of society share resources like members of one great family
- No member of society is found lacking sufficient resources for himself or herself and their family
- All members of society contribute to and bear equal responsibility for society
- A society governed by the common consent of all people
- A society of free people
- A cooperative society
- Patriarchal or traditional families with fathers providing the necessities of life and protection for their families and presiding over their families in love and righteousness and with mothers as housewives primarily responsible for nurturing their children and homemaking
- All members of society are taught universal laws, and then empowered to govern themselves.

The individual member of a good society voluntarily follows universal principles, loves other people as themselves, is selfless, and shares with other members of society.

Achieving a Good Society

Today, attempts to approximate the good society still continue, just as they have in earlier centuries. This society offers great economic validity because it deals with the greatest threat to society, which is the problem of material prosperity and greed that have been experienced throughout the history of humankind.

The key to success in fully achieving the feat of a good society is the *Law of Spirituality*. Earlier, it was stated that the members of a society must abide by universal principles in order to develop a spiritual or good society. To do this requires all members of society live the *Law of Spirituality*, because all other laws are dependent on this law. The other laws will eventually be followed as society practices the *Law of Spirituality*. If people are truly spiritual, they will love others as they do themselves, and they will share a set of values that are spiritual in nature (the *Law of Collective Values*) and their resources (the *Law of Shared Resources*) with others so no person is poor and all are equal in earthly things. The consequence (the *Law of Compliance and Collective Consequence*) of living the *Law of Spirituality,* and of this pattern of life, is happiness, peace, morality, equality, and prosperity.

The Good Society and Its Moral Economic System

The mechanism for establishing a good society today, and the solution to its social problems, is its economic system. The purposes of this economic system are to benefit all people by promoting cooperation, unity, and oneness in society and the elimination of inequality and class differences and to help the poor to prosperity through economic development and job creation. Thus, society moves toward what the English sociologist Herbert Spencer (1820-1903) called the "law of equal freedom," where people sympathize with and respect each other's claim to happiness, and thereby, everyone has the fullest freedom and greatest possible happiness.2 This would be accomplished through what can be called a "cooperative free market economic system" that is based on cooperation rather than by the present-day "free market (capitalist) economic system," or advanced capitalism, that is based on ruthless competition, or what the sociologist Amitai Etzioni calls "contained conflict," and benefits a few, as it does in the world today. This is because cooperation and trust are far more central to successful economies and other achievements than competition. People produce more in cooperation, and as a result, there is more to share. The human economy does not need to be a zero sum system in which one person's gain is another's loss as is so often assumed in capitalist economies today. Furthermore, the current materialistic capitalism fails to see to the needs of the poor and needy, and it emphasizes property rather than people.

A very similiar economic system to the "cooperative free market economic system," called the "democratic economic system," has been proposed by the economists Samuel Bowles, David M. Gordon, and Thomas E, Weisskopf in their book, *After the Waste Land.*

The "cooperative free market economic system" proposed here, is not to be confused with any form of socialism or advanced capitalism, since it calls for a system that rests on a moral base, private enterprise for (a fair) profit and the opportunity to pursue vocations by all people, exchange of goods and services relatively free from state interference, and the preservation of private property.

Socialism is based on state control and management of the economy, and to some extent, collective ownership of the means of production and distribution of goods. Of course, socialism has taken many forms today. At one extreme is China and the former governments of the Soviet Union and Eastern Europe, where repressive political systems dominate all aspects of society, including the economy. A less extreme form of socialism is found in almost all the Western European countries, particularly Sweden and Denmark, where production remains largely in private hands, but the distribution of services is centrally planned; a system that is called a welfare state. The political ideal, communism, is a form of Godless socialism that calls for all private property to be publicly owned.

Advanced capitalism, state capitalism, or materialistic capitalism, is based on essentially free markets within limits set by government policy whose purpose is suppose to benefit society as a whole, although it creates inequality, fails to care for the poor and needy, and encourages consumption. In this economic system, the means of production are privately owned and operated for "maximum" profit.

The fundamental elements for a successful cooperative economic system are: (1) moral and nonmonetary motivation, (2) full employment, (3) productive capital investment, (4) employee-owned enterprises, (5) economic responsibility, (6) equitable compensation, and (7) progressive taxation.

Moral and Nonmonetary Motivation

The most difficult hurdles in implementing a cooperative free market economy are overcoming meanness, uncaring attitudes, selfishness, pride, greed, and vested interests, and the complete acceptance and practice of advanced capitalism (that is based on profit maximization by any legal means and highly unequal rewards of income and wealth of the free market) as the natural order of life. The social commentator Steve Brouwer points out that if Americans want to counteract their social and economic ailments it will be necessary to deal with the greedy appetites of the very richest citizens and corporations who control the country's economic assets.3 It is only when a society is filled with good compassionate people with a moral value system that such a new economic system can be implemented, because it is human motivation that makes an economy operate. This requirement was probably best stated by Adam Smith (1723-1790), the Father of Free Market Economics, when he stated:

All the members of human society stand in need of each other's assistance, and are likewise exposed to mutual injuries. Where the necessary assistance is reciprocally afforded from love, from gratitude, from friendship, and esteem, the society flourishes and is happy. All the different members of it are bound together by the agreeable bonds of love and affection, and are, as it were, drawn to one common centre of mutual good offices.4

It is only by changing human attitudes and actions that such a new economic life can commence, and this happens when people understand the brother and sisterhood of all people. This realization leads to efforts to help one another and the poor, and to improve the common wealth.

Once members of society have a love and appreciation for each other and look beyond material things, they are no longer motivated by profit maximization and material success.

Full Employment

The cooperative free market economic system involves the obligation to promote the employment and training of all citizens. One of the major goals of this economy is to utilize its resources in the development of economically viable employment for all members of society. This allows the poor to become self-supporting, and in turn, allows them to help others. It is also incumbent on all members of society to work and become self-reliant. As President Franklin D. Roosevelt (1882-1945) said in his 1935 State of the Union address: "Continued dependence on relief induces a spiritual and moral disintegration fundamentally destructive to the national fiber. To dole out relief in this way is to administer a narcotic, a subtle destroyer of the human spirit."5

Productive Capital Investment

The financial institution in a cooperative economic system is charged with pooling the wealth or capital of society and reinvesting it in developing new profitable enterprises that fill economic needs. These enterprises produce new jobs and productive wealth rather than investing in speculative investments and unproductive assets, such as real estate and bonds from corporate takeovers. This economic system assigns the financial institution the function of eradicating poverty and inequality.

Employee-Owned Enterprises

Gradually all economic enterprises in a cooperative free market economy should be transformed to enterprises that offer all employees—management and labor—the opportunity to be actual owners of the enterprise, and to share in the profits of the business. Thus membership is always voluntary, however, idlers may be expelled. Modern research shows that employees who become owners and exercise job responsibility acquire the entrepreneurial spirit and display an entirely different work environment—one of cooperation. Today, the work scene is particularly characterized by the costly hostility between workers and management. One of the major earmarks of the success of the Japanese economic system until recently was the close, cooperative, and harmonious relationship between labor and management. In such participatory employee-owned organizations, all employees become owners who participate in decision making with each having one vote (the same weight) in the enterprise, such as in selecting competent managers, in job matters, and in developing company policies. Such enterprises experience increases in productivity and higher product quality, less absenteeism and turnover, higher employee morale, more profits, and the creation of new jobs.

These enterprises will utilize the different talents, skills, abilities, and training of its members. It is particularly important that the responsibility and the authority to make decisions be vested with the workers who actually do the work, resulting in workers working harder and smarter. The success of such enterprises requires all employees have access to accurate information for making intelligent decisions. No more is there a manager/worker mindset, but now all are owners, participants, and capitalists with different, but needed, and important work responsibilities.

Economic Responsibility

The members of the cooperative economy accept responsibility for the full economic ramifications of their own actions. This includes such things as the treatment of employees, working conditions, and wages. All members are also responsible for the risks and labor necessary to keep an enterprise viable. Every person is accountable for their moral enterprise. It is morality that should undergird a market place characterized by fair dealing in business matters, in buying, in selling, in a fair profit, and in general representations. This is an economic system that entrusts the economic resources to the people, not the government or a wealthy elite.

Equitable Compensation

Bowles, Gordon, and Weisskopf have found a direct correlation between economic equality and productivity growth and rate of investment.6 Yet, despite higher salaries and wages in America, the extremes in the distribution of wealth has never been greater. A comparison between the United States and Japan shows the total compensation for the chief executive officers in 1991 was 17 times as much as the average worker in Japan and 85 times as much as the average worker in the America.7 Aristotle said there should be a 5 to 1 ratio between the wealthy and poor to have a moral society.8 Peter Drucker, probably the best known economist in the world, says it should never be more than 20 to 1.9 The proposed cooperative economic system would allow differentials in earnings to provide incentives to all members of the labor force, as well as, rewards for service, training, and skill. A variety of earnings have been suggested or practiced in recent social experiments that provided a job and a decent standard of living for all members of society. These earning ratios have varied with those at the top earning between six to nine times more than those at the bottom. Limiting salary differentials in enterprises across the economic system at say, 7 to 1 is certainly more equitable when taking into consideration that each job is important and contributes to the overall operation of the enterprise and the economy, than the current over 200 to 1.

Progressive Taxation

America no longer has the system of progressive taxation that it had in the 1950s and 1960s when the United States was very strong. By the mid-1980s, the poor paid the highest overall tax rates and the rich paid the least. The effective rate of taxation on corporate profits in 1960 was 46 percent and 21 percent in 1986 while the official maximum rate of federal income tax for the richest Americans was 70 percent in 1960 and 21 percent in 1986. In 1960, the top tax rate was

91 percent and the bottom tax rate was 14 percent. Even in 1968, the top tax bracket was 75 percent and the bottom tax bracket was 14 percent. By 1993, the top bracket was only 39.6 percent and the lowest tax bracket was 15 percent. Those who benefit more from an economic system should pay a greater share of its taxes. Under a cooperative economic system, a program of progressive taxation would be instituted, although taxes in society would be substantially lowered due to greater productivity and efficiency, the gradual assumption of the responsibility for entitlements by enterprises and the private sector, the reduction in the size of government, the reduced salary differentials, and the larger tax base provided by full employment and reduced welfare and wealthfare dependency. The tax system could also be used to make it more profitable for enterprises to be creative and to discourage the use of wealth for speculative purposes.

The "Cycle of a Cooperative Free Market Economic System" is shown on the following page.

Can an economic system be made more just, fair, and humane without suppressing enterprise and drive? The answer is yes, and it can be done through a "cooperative free market economic system" based on the fundamental elements of moral and nonmonetary motivation, full employment, productive capital investment, employee-owned enterprises, economic responsibility, equitable compensation, and progressive taxation. This is an economy that has fairness and freedom. It is also an economy that promotes the general welfare and pays for itself by creating a more livable and productive society.

However, this system will succeed only with a moral people, and even then, it will require constant work to get this new economic system accepted into the hearts of all the people, since the most important national assets for any productive economy are all the members of a population.

Today, the rapidly expanding economic surpluses that have resulted from the enormous increases in productivity due to advances in technology has made numerous important social changes feasible. As Gerhard Lenski, Patrick Nolan, and Jean Lenski point out this has:

> also persuaded millions of people that things do not have to be the way they are, or the way they have always been: people have it in their power to change society and to improve social conditions. All that is needed is the will, the imagination, and a plan.10

Figure 3.3   The Cycle of a Cooperative Free Market Economic System

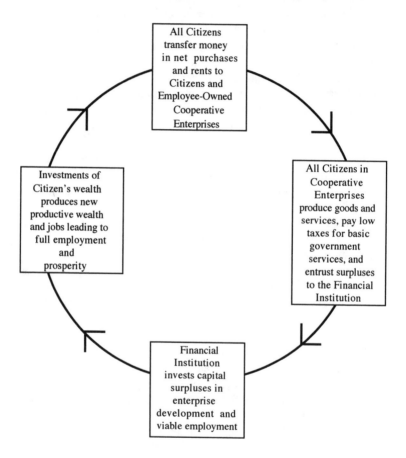

The "cooperative free market economic system" is the best alternative for improving social conditions. It is an economic system that has already been proven to be most effective in improving the economy of a community. In other words, it is beyond the experimental stage, and has been shown to achieve both economic justice and prosperity. The largest scale implementation of a prototype cooperative economic system is the extremely successful Mondragon industrial system found in the town of Mondragon in the Basque country of northern Spain. This system has operated for almost 40 years and is now a complex of over 170 cooperative enterprises employing more than 23,000 workers. It began as a small manufacturing business based on most of the fundamental elements of the cooperative economic system. Its revenues in 1990 were almost 3 billion dollars. As the attorney James Lucas and the organizational behavioralist Warner Woodworth point out:

> Research has shown that the enterprises of the Mondragon cooperative complex are more efficient, more profitable, better capitalized, and have grown faster than any comparable Spanish private firms. Retained earnings, levels of job creation, and productivity are also higher than in comparable Spanish private firms.[11]

Other smaller-scale programs that utilize the principles of a cooperative economic system have also been very successful.[12]

But as Oxford Analytica, a research and consulting firm that includes over three-hundred faculty members of Oxford University in England and other leading universities around the world, states:

> The indications are disturbing, therefore, that the dominant vision of the next decade [1990s] will most likely be one of strident individualism lacking in the idealism or moral conviction necessary to do more than muddle through. The irony of "harder times" is that pragmatism and manipulation in the pursuit of material self-interest become fashionable just when circumstances call for idealism, equity and cooperation.[13]

It is necessary for the "haves" to help the "have nots" and enhance them, otherwise, they or their children will eventually suffer the same fate of the "have nots." The author Steve Brouwer further states, "We have a choice: a degenerating world dominated by the rich, or a rich and prospering world that belongs to everyone."[14]

The sociologist Denny Braun also states:

> In the final analysis, every person in our society should be able to lead a productive life free from want. We need to guarantee that each American has the basic health care, food, and shelter to survive. This can be accomplished if we are willing to use the power that has been within us all along.15

This is possible if people will use their power to implement the Good Society and its moral economic system.

Chapter 11

The Restoration of America

America will probably never celebrate a 300th birthday! There is a far greater war facing the American Republic today than the American War for Independence. It is a war against American materialism, and the stakes are high. America could collapse within a generation if it continues to follow the materialistic road.

But there is still time to confront this social crisis described in chapter 3, and prevent America's ruin. These materialistic trends can just as easily be reversed as allowed to continue—and in a generation, too. It will be the citizens of America who decide what to do, if anything.

For any decision and action to be taken first requires the recognition of the crisis. Just as an alcoholic must recognize there is a problem before he or she can begin to solve it, so to, the American people must fully recognize they are faced with the most serious social crisis in America's history before they can begin to correct it, because the first step begins with them. The debate about whether we have a real crisis seems to be over. The real question of the moment is whether people will be willing to save themselves. The members of society must now resolve to change, for they are society and a society has no mind of its own, only that of its membership.

There seems to be a genuine desire on the part of many people to find out what is wrong in America, and to do something about it. However, it will require sacrifice. Recent efforts just at government budget deficit reduction indicate that Americans give lip service to sacrifice, but when it comes to doing it they always want the other guy to sacrifice, and that will not work. It will take a call to "equitable" sacrifice with all sharing the burden.

What do we do about it? How do we solve this tremendous social crisis? No one knows with certainty the answer to this question. A few have proposed causes and/or solutions. For example, the political philosopher Francis Fukuyama suggests that the loss of social groups based on human trust and obligation or a trusting community is the cause of a nation's decline in civic life.1 David Blankenhorn sees the decline of the family as linked to the decline of other institutions in a civil society, and of society.2 The American Enterprise Institute scholar, Charles Murray, also sees the breakdown of the family as the most important social problem of our time, and the one that drives all other problems.3 The late Christopher Lasch sees a new intellectual or cultural elite as the cause of America's moral foundering.4 The management specialist Peter Drucker also sees America's working world going through a social transformation that pits privileged knowledge workers against everyone else.5 John A. Howard sees the resurrection of wisdom or the understanding of what will be of benefit to everyone as necessary to reconstitute decent, moral, and lawful societies.6 Mancur Olson explains the rise and decline of nations as a result of the compromising of state autonomy.7 The historian Paul Kennedy argues that large military expenditures will cause the decline of America.8 Princeton's Robert Wuthnow sees the loss of moral underpinnings or values, not economic conditions, threatening America today.9 The journalist and author Haynes Johnson found racial and ethic tensions and economic inequities inevitably resulting in greater problems in America.10 Robert Bellah believes most of America's problems come from the market economy.11 It is William Bennett, Robert Bork, and the evangelist Billy Graham who recognize that the real crisis in America is spiritual.12

These are only a few examples, from many, of the ways offered to explain the decline of American society, but they are incomplete and/or devoid of a plan. This study explains what has happened to America, and what is required to change its course of destruction. All recent proposals except three have failed to recognize the first law, the *Law of Collective Spirituality*. Those religious leaders besides Graham, who do recognize it, are usually not heard.

The Keys to Restoring America

Restoring America will not be easy. To be sure, the level of spirituality is sufficient for only a beginning, but the seeds are there for a spiritual transformation, and eventually, a complete recovery.

The three keys to restoring America are a return to spirituality, strengthening the family, and instituting equality by transforming the economic system. To accomplish these three restoring goals, all American people must develop a sense of community and be united in purpose like at no other time in America's history in order to defeat the common but seldom recognized enemy within, the enemy of materialism. They must also exhibit self-restraint and make great sacrifices. To meet the goal of restoring America will require a plan.

An Initial Plan for Restoring America

The plan for restoring America calls for major changes in the five major institutions: religion, family, economy, education, and government. Only if America begins making these changes will a catastrophe be averted. We should heed the words of John Winthrop (1588-1649), the first governor of Massachusetts Bay Colony, in 1630 as he spoke to a little band of Pilgrims on the deck of the tiny Arabella about the life they would have in a new land they had never seen. He said:

> We shall be a city upon a hill. The eyes of all people are upon us, so that if we shall deal falsely with our God in this work we have undertaken, and so cause Him to withdraw His present help from us, we shall be made a story and a byword through the world.13

Religion

The Founding Fathers of America acknowledged God in the founding and preservation of this country, something that later generations of Americans have forgotten. This was expressed by John Adams, before signing the Declaration, when he said, "There's a divinity that shapes our ends."14 The Founding Fathers declared God to be the ultimate authority for their basis of law. After the Constitution was done, The Father of the Constitution, James Madison (1751-1836) wrote: "It is impossible for the man of pious reflection not to perceive in it a finger of that Almighty hand which has been so frequently and signally extended to our relief in the critical stage of the revolution."15 George Washington (1732-1799) referred to the creation of the Constitution as a "miracle."16

Washington and Benjamin Franklin (1706-1790) both declared that America must include prayer in its national life if it is going to maintain prosperity and success.17 In his Farewell Address Washington, the first president of the United States, warned:

> Of all the dispositions and habits which lead to political prosperity, religion and morality are indispensable supports ... And let us with caution indulge the supposition that morality can be maintained without religion ... reason and experience both forbid us to expect that national morality can prevail in exclusion of religious principle.18

Franklin warned the nation that the exclusion of God would result in America experiencing internal disputes, the decay of the nation's prestige and reputation, and a diminished national success.19 John Adams (1735-1826) said that the "Constitution was made only for a moral and religious people, it is wholly inadequate for the government of any other."20

The importance of God to America is expressed in The National Anthem, in our coins, and in the Pledge of Allegiance. One of the loveliest hymns sung by the citizens of America is "My Country, 'Tis of Thee." This hymn expresses gratitude to God for liberty and voices a prayer that He will continue to bless America with the holy light of freedom. Throughout American history belief in God recurs with regularity and prominence.

Where did America's spirituality go? Well, despite an extended history of God in America, He was officially removed in 1962 and 1963 from the daily lives of citizens with the removal of prayer and Bible-reading in the public schools, and subsequently, other religious principles. America stopped acknowledging God.

The ramifications of this event on America's spirituality was studied by David Barton. His findings are described in his book *America: To Pray or Not to Pray.*21 Barton in comparing statistics on the prayer years with the post-prayer years (from 1951 to 1986) identifies strong evidence that only one item, the banning of prayer, was associated with a distinct and well-defined new direction of 15 to 20 consecutive years of uninterrupted decay in America beginning in 1963. The areas of decay concerning students include student academics, student premarital sexual activity, teen pregnancies, sexually transmitted diseases among teens, student suicide rates and drug use. The areas of decay for family breakups include divorce, single-parent families, runaways, cohabitation, adultery, and the physical and sexual abuse of children. He found the same trends true of measurements concerning the nation in the areas of crime, productivity, alcohol use, public corruption, AIDS, and illiteracy. He uncovered many new problems appearing on the national scene after 1963 including child abuse, corruption among public officials, drug use, AIDS, and illiteracy. This decay continues to this day.

Today, the elite culture has privatized faith and pushed it to the margins of society by acting on unspoken shared assumptions that religion is backward, medieval, embarrassing or irrelevant.

However, Alexis de Tocquiville, the Frenchman who observed America in the 19th Century said:

> Not until I went to the churches of America and heard her pulpits aflame with righteousness did I understand the secret of her genius and power. America is great because she is good, and if America ever ceases to be good, America will cease to be great.22

Angus McDonald (1904-1990), the founder and editor of *The St. Crois Review,* wrote in 1967:

> From the founding of this country until some time after the war of Revolution, our thinking was dominated by religious precepts ... But the clear and certain faith that religious precepts should rule society has been absent for the lifetime of every living American ... The problem of society was to live in the everyday world by principles derived from a superior world. That wisdom has been lost ...23

Most importantly, America must have a spiritual core to overcome its social crisis. What can be done?

First, practice moral principles in personal daily lives.

Second, pray to God or a supreme being or higher power.

Third, develop faith in God or the supreme being.

Fourth, read holy writings and scriptures with a sincere effort to regain what the Founding Fathers knew.

Fifth, read good books that teach values.

Sixth, enroll children in religious training.

Seventh, attend undefiled churches and church activities that teach such values as morality, decency, respect for others, patriotism, and honoring and sustaining the law.

Eighth, look for the purposes of life and death and humanity's destiny after death by reading materials from the study of near-death experiences or of those who have died and returned to tell others what they learned about it.

Ninth, develop attitudes of selflessness and charity.

Tenth, parents should teach and instill in their children the time-honored values of honesty, integrity, industry, service, to esteem one another as God's children, social tolerance, and love, and then, set an example by living them.

Eleventh, rebuild the shared moral values of communities across the country.

Twelfth, reinstate prayer and religion in America's national life.

These are some beginning steps that Americans can use to begin to restore a higher power in life and a return to spirituality both privately and publicly.

Family

There is no society that can endure for any length of time the destruction of the family. Unless society learns how to revalue marriage and restigmatize broken relations between mothers and fathers, the empirical evidence suggests that marriage declines, and so does fatherhood and society too. America's families must be strengthened! The following are some beginning steps in this process:

First, reinstitute the traditional nuclear family as the "pillar of society" just as the old Soviet Union did in its failed family experiment earlier in the century.

Second, strengthen family authority and return the father to the head of the family.

Third, teach the nation that parenting is important, and a full-time and crucial work for preparing the nation's future.

Fourth, mothers with young children should be encouraged to stay home with their children.

Fifth, make divorce more difficult to obtain. All legal rulings on divorce should be based on the best interests of society, not the individual.

Sixth, families must assume their responsibility for teaching children moral behavior and other virtues primarily through increased interaction with their children and by example. (For example, families could buy and begin reading together the *Bible* or *The Book of Virtues* by William Bennett.)

Seventh, stop abortions except in cases where the life of the mother is in danger.

Eighth, supervise the television viewing of children, which sends messages of violence, consumption of alcohol, poor nutrition, opulent lifestyles and materialism, family diversity, and immorality.

Ninth, take actions to stop by law and by not viewing or hearing the filth (such as murder, violence, nudity, sex, and profanity), moral degradation, and values that are portrayed in all forms of entertainment by most media people, who are ignorant of religion and in discord with the public. Do not tolerate trash for the sake of art. [The 19th Century English critic John Ruskin (1819-1900) said, "Taste is not only a part and an index of morality—it is the only morality. The first, and last, and closest trial question to any living creature is, 'What do you like?' Tell me what you like, and I'll tell you what you are."24 In this century, Edith Hamilton, a noted author on Greek and Roman civilizations has said that the best indication of what the people of any period are like is the plays they go to see. Popular drama shows the public quality like nothing else.25 (Popular drama also helps to perpetuate the values it shows.)]

Tenth, teach children that sexual relations outside marriage are wrong instead of offering them free birth-control devices, easy access to abortion, and massive doses of sex education.

Eleventh, give children responsibilities and keep them away from unlimited fun and frolic.

Twelfth, enforce laws regulating sexual relations including ending the support for illegitimacy.

Thirteenth, stop rewarding fatherless families by reformulating welfare laws.

Economy

America can actually afford to have no poor people as well as provide a fairly comfortable life for all its citizens. Economic inequality is helping to destroy this reality. It is also dividing America. As mentioned previously, economic inequality is the best indicator of materialism in a society, and it is the cause of social conflict and destruction. Advanced capitalist economies create inequalities of ownership and income, and require public policies to correct these abuses and encourage a gradual transformation of the traditional economic system to a cooperative free market economic system. The following are some initial steps to change the disastrous effect of traditional advanced capitalism and the spreading gap between rich and poor:

First, institute a fair and equitable progressive tax system so that everyone contributes according to the share of society's resources they receive and their financial ability, and so that economic inequality is dramatically reduced. (The American economy thrived in the face of much higher taxes on well-off families during the 1950s and 1960s.)

Second, lower the tax burden of all citizen's to encourage productivity and full prosperity.

Third, institute progressively higher estate and inheritance taxes in order to engage all members of society in productive work.

Fourth, balance the budget and pay off the national debt.

Fifth, for the present time institute a guaranteed income level for society so all people can live without poverty, hunger, and homelessness.

Sixth, reformulate welfare laws and begin returning people to work by ministering to the spiritual side of people, getting them to accept responsibility for choices, job training, and job opportunities.

Seventh, reduce all extravagant consumption.

Eighth, reduce consumption of foreign products in order to balance foreign trade.

Ninth, establish life-long learning programs for all workers and the financial assistance for program participation.

Tenth, award a higher education to academically qualified applicants and students in good standing.

Eleventh, provide a job for every able-bodied worker, even through public work programs if necessary.

Twelfth, invest in civilian research and development.

Thirteenth, aggressively enforce laws against organizations who operate illegally in obtaining money and profits.

Fourteenth, invest in rebuilding the industrial and national infrastructure.

Fifteenth, volunteer time and money to help the poor and build communities.

Sixteenth, consider instituting a full or partial loan debt forgiveness program.

Seventeenth, reduce the interest rates.

Eighteenth, move toward a cooperative free market economic system nationally as expeditiously as possible.

Education

The education system can be used to reinforce efforts for change in other social institutions. Here are some proposed initial steps to follow:

First, return to teaching the basics in the schools.

Second, reinstate prayer and remove hostility towards religion in the schools.

Third, stop teaching the new ethic in the public schools and return to teaching traditional values and providing a moral education.

Fourth, use proven techniques of learning, and stop flirting with unproven experiments and faddish methods of teaching and learning.

Fifth, equip and furnish all schools equitably.

Sixth, vote support for justified school budgets.

Seventh, restore discipline to the schools.

Eighth, maintain strict educational and grading standards at all levels of education including higher education.

Ninth, let teachers teach.

Tenth, have schools assist in teaching job skills.

Eleventh, raise teacher salaries to attract the best citizens to teaching.

Government

Government must be active and not stalemated; it must be a "spiritual democracy." As President Dwight D. Eisenhower (1890-

1969) put it: "Our government makes no sense unless it is founded in a deeply felt religious faith—and I don't care what it is."26 President George Washington said in his first inaugural address that "Of all the dispositions and habits that lead to political prosperity, religion and morality are indispensable supports."27 President John F. Kennedy (1917-1963) also described the dependence of the political order on the religious order when he stated in his inaugural address: "The rights of man come not from the generosity of the state but from the hand of God."28 America critically needs a sense of purpose and the leadership that will bring people together to meet this purpose. Several steps can be followed to begin this process:

First, elect people who can clearly articulate the social crisis America faces and a plan to meet this crisis.

Second, elect people who have some transcendent sense of why they are in government and what has to be done to restore America.

Third, elect good, honest, wise, uncorrupted, and well-intended people to government offices who will do what is best for all the people, not a select few.

Fourth, elect "servants" of the people, not "monarchs" who serve themselves and their own interests and the special interests of the rich, and put themselves above the people and the law.

Fifth, elect "servants" of the people to serve a term limit with only the expenses of service to be covered.

Sixth, allow the opportunity for any good candidate for office to run by setting up limited election funds for elected offices and prohibiting all financial contributions, and thereby, removing money and political favors from elections and public service in order to break the stranglehold of the rich on government and the economy so these institutions serve all the people. (Usually, the best candidates are not running for elective office.)

Seventh, outlaw PACs, lobbyists, and political gifts.

Eighth, stop wasteful spending of the taxpayer's money.

Ninth, reduce government regulation and control (this will tend to increase economic growth).

Tenth, legislate laws that reflect traditional morality.

Eleventh, allocate equitable federal funding to the states, and from the states, to the counties, and from the counties, to the communities and wards for the most efficient and effective use of funds to state and community problems and priorities.

Twelfth, resuscitate community civic life through stronger local government and funding decisions and community planning for the future.

Thirteenth, stop foreign aid and space exploration and use the funding to care for the poor and rebuild the nation. (America should take care of its own house first, and then assist the world and explore space.)

Fourteenth, reduce military spending to the level necessary for the defense of the nation, or by at least 200 billion dollars annually. [(Now, America has a 300 billion dollars or more investment on machinery and employees that cannot produce anything of value for the rest of the economy.) (Paul Kennedy has argued that Spain, Great Britain, and Germany fell from preeminent world positions when the cost of their empires and the projecting their military power exceeded the strength of their economies. He sees a decline of America's economy as it continues the expensive effort of maintaining a world military presence.29 The sociologist Paul Blumberg proposes that a permanent war economy contributes to a crisis of American capitalism too.30 Denny Braun states: "The more a nation spends on its military, the lower its investment productivity, and civilian research and development tends to be."31)]

Fifteenth, stop policing the world. (This is a job for the world community to share.)

Sixteenth, let all the people vote on the most major issues facing the nation and share in the responsibility for their resolution. (This is technologically feasible now.)

Benjamin Franklin once said to the nation, "Do you want to be a world leader? Then put Christian principles in your public affairs."32 This is essentially what is called for in many of the steps of this proposed initial plan to restore America. Truly, these principles and steps can begin to return America to spirituality, strengthen its families, institute equality, and lift America from its social crisis. As the *Bible* states, "Righteousness exalted a nation...." (Prov. 14:34), and it is the spiritual road that will exalt and restore America.

Chapter 12

Some Thoughts on Global Society

History shows that complex civilizations always lose their spirituality and become unequal, and so far, they have always succumbed to the problems generated by their unspiritualness and inequality.

Kenneth McFarland, an educator, listed six common reasons why civilizations fail:

1. They lose their religious convictions and flouted basic morality.
2. They become obsessed with sex.
3. They debase their money of its intrinsic value and let inflation run rampant.
4. Honest work ceases to be a virtue.
5. Respect for law disintegrates and violence becomes an accepted method of achieving individual and group desires.
6. Finally, citizens are no longer willing to be soldiers and fight for the defense of their nation and their heritage.[1]

The English author, C. S. Lewis (1898-1963), addresses particularly spirituality in the collapse of civilizations when he wrote:

What Satan put into the heads of our remote ancestors was the idea that they ... could ... invent some sort of happiness for themselves outside God, apart from God. And out of that hopeless attempt has come nearly all that we call human history—money, poverty, ambition, war, prostitution, classes, empires, slavery—the long terrible story of man trying to find something other than God which will make him happy....

That is the key to history. Terrific energy is expended—civilizations are built up—excellent institutions devised; but each time something goes wrong. Some fatal flaw always brings the selfish and cruel people to the top and it all slides back into misery and ruin. In fact, the machine conks. It seems to start up all right and runs a few years, and then it breaks down. They are trying to run it on the wrong juice. That is what Satan has done to us humans.2

Will Durant further elaborates on the failure of the Great Roman Empire when he writes:

A great civilization is not conquered from without until it has destroyed itself within. The essential causes of Rome's decline lay in her people, her morals, her class struggle, her failing trade, her bureaucratic despotism, her stifling taxes, her consuming wars.3

The linguist, classicist, and historian Hugh Nibley similarly adds:

Some civilizations have been destroyed by plague, some by upheavals of nature, some by invading armies, some by exhaustion of natural resources. Whatever the ultimate cause, the decline and fall was usually accompanied by a weakening of moral and mental fiber rendering the society progressively less capable of meeting progressively mounting dangers.4

The late novelist Walker Percy (1916-1990) when asked what concerned him the most about the future of American civilization, said:

Probably the fear of seeing America, with all its great strength and beauty and freedom ... gradually subside into decay through default and be defeated, not by the Communist movement ... but from within by weariness, boredom, cynicism, greed and in the end helplessness before its great problems.5

However, never before in the history of humankind and American civilization has there been so much potential for a world free of decay, suffering, and unhappiness because of the technology and productivity possible through free market capitalism. Technology has given humanity the possibility of a social order with greater freedom, justice, and happiness than has ever been known. Perhaps one of the biggest economic megatrends of the times is the global expansion of capitalism. Throughout Latin America, Eastern Europe, Russia, China, India, and other Asian nations, economic growth and capitalism are accelerating at a remarkable pace.

Today, there is a movement toward a so-called global society because modern societies have so many ties with other societies resulting in the fate of all societies being linked with the fate of the world. But, if people look at the world, with its ever more interrelated activities, they will find a world with a merging economic system and a stratification system that is very similar to the domestic system of stratification in America. America's class structure is a microcosm of the world's class structure. In other words, people will find a world divided into something similar to classes with their differing interests, resulting in hidden and open class conflict.

It is a world that is continuing to witness a widening gap between rich and poor countries with an income gulf between rich and poor individuals around the world of more than 140 to 1 in 1992 as compared to America's gap of 12 to 1. The top 1 percent of income recipients in the world receives about 15 percent of worldwide income and the top 5 percent of recipients gets 40 percent of all income. On the other hand, the poorest 20 percent of the world's population get only 1 percent of global income. This income gap between the richest 20 percent and the poorest 20 percent of the world's population has doubled since 1960. This gap between rich and poor is continuing to widen around the globe today, resulting in the world becoming more economically polarized, both between countries and within countries. This is despite the fact that generally the world's economy has been surging. The administrator of the United Nations Development Program, James Gustave Speth, wrote: "If present trends continue, economic disparities between industrial and developing nation will move from inequitable to inhuman."6 As this inequality gets worse between nations, income inequality within nations also tends to grow.

Simply put, this means there is not only a tremendous possibility for a world free of decay, suffering, and unhappiness as never before in history, but also an overwhelming likelihood for a collapse of world civilization as we know it.

Daniel Rossides has stated that "domestic power structures that do not provide for the equitable distribution of the fruits of social life are the major cause of the world's troubles."7 He adds that world problems, including the threat of war, have resulted from imperialist actions of societies over the past centuries as power groups struggled to make their inequitable societies work.

Today, there is a developing dual world, or a growing polarization in the world, consisting of rich and poor that can lead to a financial crisis and collapse of the capitalist world economy and the world's social structure, just as it is happening in America, unless some curative steps are taken, and soon. What is called for is a worldwide spiritual reawakening and regeneration and a transformation of the global economy.

The universal social principles provide for the understanding of this global development. The keys to creating a new world are a return to spirituality, a strengthening of the family, and instituting equality by transforming the world's economic system to a worldwide cooperative free market economic system. The world's people will also have to develop a sense of community and be united in purpose to overcome the evils of materialism and selfishness. They must also be willing to share and have charity and concern for each other. They must recognize there is no need for competitive accumulation of the earth's wealth and resources, for there is enough for all the earth's inhabitants to share despite what the pessimists say. As a popular song says, "what the world needs now, is love sweet love."

All humankind needs to remember the wise words of Chief Seattle (1786?-1866) in his testimony of 1854:

... All things are connected.

This we know. The earth does not belong to man,
Man belongs to the earth.
This we know. All things are connected like the blood
which unites one family.
All things are connected.

Whatever befalls the earth befalls the sons of the earth.
Man did not weave the web of life, he is merely a strand in it.
Whatever he does to the web, he does to himself.8

In the article, "The State of Greed," is clearly stated humanity's biggest challenge in the dawning of the Twenty-First Century:

Perhaps the biggest challenge of the first years of the 21st century will be making sure that the blessings of money—the freedoms it allows, the achievements it nourishes, the sense of stewardship it inspires—don't turn into darker forces that shrivel humanity.9

What will humanity do with their blessings of money? Can we expect men and women in America and in the world at the dawning of the Twenty-First Century to usher in an age of spiritualness, a new "Great Awakening," by rejecting the darker forces? Will humanity be wise enough to heed the univerisal principles of life? Only time can answer these questions.

Appendix

Theoretical Comparisons

The following theoretical comparisons are presented to assist students of society in their study of differences and similarities between social theories of society. For purposes of comparison, the theory or explanation proposed in this book will be referred to as "unified humanity theory." Although the comparisons are made at different levels of analysis because those theories of society that are most widely recognized today are not unified theories but rather are either micro-level theories or macro-level theories. There have not been any attempts until this book to develop a unified theory in sociology for over 30 years. The development of a meso-level theory has only recently begun, and no particular theory is widely accepted yet.

On the other hand, the unified humanity theory is a comprehensive or unified theory that encompasses all levels of analysis—micro, meso, and macro levels. Central assumptions of the theory are identified at the micro and macro levels for the purpose of this comparison.

The first comparison is shown under the title, "A Simple Comparsion of the Major Assumptions of Symbolic Interactionism and Unified Humanity Theory." This shows a theoretical perspective known as symbolic interactionism that attempts to understand social life from the viewpoint of the individual. This perspective is called micro-level theory. It was initially developed by the sociologists Max Weber and George Simmel and later sociologists such as Charles

Horton Cooley, George Herbert Mead, W. I. Thomas, Erving Goffman, Harold Garfinkel, and Herbert Blumer contributed to the further development of this perspective. This comparison outlines the most basic assumptions found in symbolic interactionism and compares them with those found at this level of analysis in unified humanity theory. However, as you may realize from studying the unified humanity theory in this book, unified humanity theory locates the basic assumptions of symbolic interactionism at the meso level of analysis rather than at the micro level of analysis.

The second comparison is shown under the title, "A Simple Comparison of the Major Assumptions of Functionalism, Conflict Theory, and Unified Humanity Theory." This comparison outlines the basic assumptions of functionalism, conflict theory, and unified humanity theory and compares them with one another. This comparison examines the perspective that is called macro-level theory. The major contributors to the functionlist perspective were Herbert Spencer and Emile Durkheim. In recent years, Talcott Parsons, Robert Merton, Kingsley Davis, and Wilbert Moore contributed to this theory. The sociologists who initially developed the conflict perspective were Karl Marx, Max Weber, and George Simmel. They were followed by later contributors to this perspective that included C. Wright Mills, Ralf Dahrendorf, and Randall Collins.

Since stratification in society is such a central part of the unified humanity theory, the final two comparisons contrast the views of the macro-level theories on the stratification of society. The first of these comparisons is titled, "A Simple Comparison of Four Models of Social Stratification." This comparison includes a theory known as evolutionary theory that was proposed by sociologist Gerhard Lenski in the 1960s. This theory was an attempt by Lenski to develop a new theory by uniting and synthesizing various features of functional and conflict theories and combinding them with some of his own theoretical ideas. The second of these comparisons outlines the assumptions of conflict, functionalist, and unified humanity theory views of stratification and indicates any overlaping between the views of unified humanity theory with the functional and conflict views. It is titled, "Conflict, Functionalist, and Unified Humanity Theory Views of Social Stratification: A Comparison."

Table A.1   A   Simple   Comparison   of   the   Major   Assumptions   of   Symbolic   Interactionism   and   Unified   Humanity   Theory

Symbolic Interactionism[1]	Unified Humanity Theory
1. Human beings act according to their own interpretations of reality.	1. Human beings act according to their thoughts that are based on personal values and motives.
2. Subjective interpretations are based on the meanings we learn from others.	2. Human social actions are influenced by the social forces of society.
3. Human beings are constantly interpreting their own behavior as well as the behavior of others in terms of learned symbols and meanings.	3. Human social interaction occurs with the exchange of culturally established meanings primarily through language between individuals who occupy social positions in society.
	4. Human social interaction is guided by individual values and perceptions of social reality.
	5. Human beings are constantly interpreting their own behavior as well as the behavior of others in terms of learned symbols and meanings.

[1] SOURCE: Jon M. Shepard, *Sociology,* 5th ed. (St. Paul, Minnesota: West Publishing Company, 1993), p. 32.

Table A.2   A Simple Comparison of the Major Assumptions of Functionalism, Conflict Theory, and Unified Humanity Theory

Functionalism[1]	Conflict Theory[1]	Unified Humanity Theory
1. A society is a relatively integrated whole.	1. A society experiences inconsistency and conflict everywhere.	1. A society is united or divided depending on its distribution of resources.
2. A society tends to seek relative stability or dynamic equilibrium.	2. A society is continually subjected to change everywhere.	2. A society is subjected to change when the spirituality or material pursuits of its members change.
3. Most elements of a society contribute to the society's well-being and survival.	3. Elements of a society tend to contribute to the society's instability.	3. The institutions or elements of a society can either contribute to the society's well-being and survival or to its decline.
4. A society rests on the consensus of its members.	4. A society rests on the constraint and coercion of some of its members by others.	4. A society rests on the spirituality and core values of its collective membership to determine the relations of its members.

[1]SOURCE: Jon M. Shepard, *Sociology*, 5th ed. (St. Paul, Minnesota: West Publishing Company, 1993), p. 32.

Table A.3   A Simple Comparison of Four Models of Social Stratification

Basis of Comparison1	Conflict Theory1	Functional Theory1	Evolutionary Theory1	Unified Humanity Theory
Society can best be understood as ...	Groups competing for scarce resources	Groups cooperating to meet common needs	Exhibiting cooperation as well as conflict	Cooperating or competing dependent on societal type (divided or united)
Social structures can best be understood as patterns that ...	Maintain current patterns of inequality	Solve problems and help society adapt	Help solve problems, but help some groups more than others	Range from helping to meet needs of society's members equally to maintaining patterns of inequality
Causes of stratification are ...	Unequal control of means of production maintained by force, fraud, and trickery	Importance of vital tasks; unequal ability	Need for coordination giving some people power, which they use to amass privilege	Materialistic values and pursuits by members of society
Conclusion about stratification ...	Difficult to eliminate, but unnecessary and undesirable	Necessary and desirable	Necessary under conditions of low surplus; currently much more inequality than is necessary or desirable	Can be eliminated, and unnecessary and undesirable

1SOURCE: David B. Brinkerhoff and Lynn K. White, *Sociology*, 2nd ed. (St. Paul, Minnesota: West Publishing Company, 1988), p. 224.

Table A.4   **Conflict, Functionalist, and Unified Humanity Theory Views of Social Stratification: A Comparison**

Conflict View

1. Stratification may be universal without being necessary or inevitable.
2. The stratification system shapes social organizations (the social system).
3. Stratification arises from group conquest, competition, and conflict.
4. Stratification impedes the optimal functioning of society and the individual.
5. Stratification is an expression of the values of powerful groups.
6. Power is usually illegitimately distributed in society.
7. Tasks and rewards are inequitably allocated.
8. The economic dimension is paramount in society.
9. Stratification systems often change through revolutionary processes.

Functionalist View

1. Stratification is universal, necessary, and inevitable.
2. Social organization (the social system) shapes the stratification system.
3. Stratification arises from the societal need for integration, coordination, and cohesion.
4. Stratification facilitates the optimal functioning of society and the individual.
5. Stratification is an expression of commonly shared social values.
6. Power is usually legitimately distributed in society.
7. Tasks and rewards are equitably allocated.
8. The economic dimension is subordinate to other dimensions of society.
9. Stratification systems generally change through evolutionary processes.

Unified Humanity Theory View

1. Stratification may be universal without being necessary or inevitable (also Conflict View)
2. Spiritual or materialistic pursuits of the members of society shape its social structure.
3. Stratification arises from materialism.
4. Stratification impedes the optimal functioning of society and the individual, and can destroy society. (similar to Conflict View)
5. Stratification is an expression of the values and behavior of members of society. (similar to Functionalist View)
6. Power is distributed according to wealth and power in a stratified society. (similar to Conflict View)
7. Tasks and rewards are inequitably allocated in a stratified society. (similar to Conflict View)
8. The spiritual (or religious) dimension is paramount in society.
9. Stratification systems change as the collective values of society's members change and can do so in as short a time as a generation.

Endnotes

Chapter 1: Introduction

1. John Naisbitt and Patricia Aburdene, *Megatrends 2000* (New York: William Morrow and Company, Inc., 1990), p. 12.

Chapter 2: Overview

1. Johathan H. Turner and Leonard Beeghley, *The Emergence of Sociological Theory* (Chicago: The Dorsey Press, 1981), p. 38.

Chapter 3: The State of America

1. John Leo, "Confronting the Social Deficit," *U.S. News & World Report,* February 8, 1993, p. 28.
2. Alexander Pope, *An Essay on Man,* epistle i, 1. 217.
3. *The Index of Social Health 1991: Monitoring the Social Well-Being of the Nation* (Tarrytown, New York: Fordham Institute for Innovation in Social Policy, 1991).
4. William Bennett, *The Index of Leading Cultural Indicators* (Washington, D.C.: Heritage Foundation, 1993).
5. "Low-Income People Show Generosity," *El Paso Times,* October 19, 1988.
6. Steve Brouwer, *Sharing the Pie: A Disturbing Picture of the U.S. Economy* (Carlisle, Pennsylvania: Big Picture Books, n.d.), p. 44.
7. Michael J. Gerson, "Do Do-gooders Do Much Good," *U.S. News & World Report,* April 28, 1997, p. 27.

8. Harold R. Kerbo, *Social Stratification and Inequality: Class Conflict in Historical and Comparative Perspective,* 2nd ed. (New York: McGraw-Hill, 1991), pp. 102-104.

9. Daniel E. Rossides, *Social Stratification: The American Class System in Comparative Perspective* (Englewood Cliffs, New Jersey: Prentice Hall, 1990), pp. 471-493.

10. John Leo, "Sneer not at 'Ozzie and Harriet,'" *U.S. News & World Report,* September 14, 1992, p. 24.

11. *Rebuilding the Nest: A New Commitment to the American Family,* eds. David Blankenhorn, Steven Bayme, and Jean Bethke Elshtain (Milwaukee, Wisconsin: Family Service America, 1990), pp. 39-51.

12. Denny Braun, *The Rich Get Richer: The Rise of Income Inequality in the United States and the World* (Chicago: Nelson Hall, Inc., 1991), p. 1.

13. Barbara Ehrenreich, "Is the Middle Class Doomed?" *New York Times Magazine,* September 5-11, 1988, p. 63.

14. John Liscio, "Uncle Sam as Robin Hood," *U.S. News & World Report,* June 1, 1992, p. 53.

15. Jon M. Shepard, *Sociology,* 5th ed. (St. Paul, Minnesota: West Publishing Company, 1993), pp. 45-46.

16. *Ibid.,* p. 46.

17. See Leonard Silk, "The End of the Road?" *New York Times Book Review,* a review of Robert L. Heilbroner, *Business Civilization in Decline* (New York: Nolton, 1976).

18. Harrison Rainie with Margaret Loftus and Mark Madden, "The State of Greed," *U.S. News & World Report,* June 17, 1996, pp. 64, 67.

19. Ann Landers, "Are College Kids as Bad As all That," *El Paso Times,* December 8, 1991, p. 4F.

20. Robert H. Bork, *Slouching Towards Gomorrah: Modern Liberalism and American Decline* (New York: HarperCollins Publishers, Inc., 1996). pp. 158, 170.

21. John Leo, "A Pox on Dan and Murphy," *U.S. News & World Report,* June 1, 1992, p. 19.

22. David Blankenhorn, *Fatherless America: Confronting Our Most Urgent Social Problem* (New York: Basic Books, 1995).

23. Daniel Patrick Moynihan, *Family and Nation* (New York: Harcourt Brace Jovanovich Publishers, 1987), p. 9.

24. John A. Howard, an Address Delivered at the 25th Anniversary of *The St. Croix Review* and the Journal's Founder and Editor Angus McDonald, October 21, 1992.

25. *Ibid.*

26. Rainie with Loftus and Madden, *op. cit.,* p. 67.

27. Neal A. Maxwell, "Deny Yourselves of all Ungodliness," *Ensign,* May, 1995, p. 67.

28. William J. Bennett, "Quantifying America's Decline," *Wall Street Journal,* March 15, 1993.

29. Daniel Bell, *The Cultural Contradiction of Capitalism* (New York: Basic Books, 1976), p. 481.

Chapter 4: The Universal Social Principles of Life

1. Tamotsu Shibutani, *Social Processes: An Introduction to Sociology* (Berkeley: University of California Press, 1986), p. 68.

2. Richard W. Wetherill, *Tower of Babel* (Wynnewood, Pennsylvania: 1952).

3. Emil F. Smidak, *Smidak Principles* (Granges-Paccot, Switzerland: Institute of Federalism, University of Fribourg, 1994).

4. John J. Macionis, *Society: The Basics,* 3rd ed. (Upper Saddle River, New Jersey: Prentice Hall, 1996), p. 87.

5. David Lawrence, "Someday—a Real Christmas," *U.S. News & World Report,* December 27, 1982/January 3, 1983, pp. 87-88.

6. William Shakespeare, "Two Gentlemen of Verona," *The Complete Works of William Shakespeare* (New York: Avenel Books, 1975), p. 25.

7. Morton Deutsch, *The Resolution of Conflict* (New Haven, Connecticut: Yale University Press, 1973).

8. Florence Scovel Shinn, *The Game of Life and How to Play It* (Del Rey, California: Devorss Publications, 1925).

Chapter 5: The Spiritual Factor: The Forgotten Factor and The Determinant of Societal and Personal Destiny

1. Will Durant and Ariel Durant, *The Lessons of History* (New York: Simon and Schuster, 1968), p. 51.

2. James Patterson and Peter Kim, *The Day America Told the Truth* (New York: Penguin Book USA Inc., 1991), p. 235.

3. A similar treatment of spirituality is found in Dallin H. Oaks, *Pure in Heart* (Salt Lake City, Utah: Bookcraft, Inc., 1988).

4. Robert Nisbet, *The Present Age* (New York: Harper and Row, 1988), pp. 134-135.

5. Max Weber, *The Protestant Ethic and the Spirit of Capitalism* (New York: Charles Scribners Sons, 1958).

6. Friedrich Nietzche, *The Philosophy of Nietzsche* (New York: Random House, Inc., 1954), p. 6.

7. Emile Durkheim, *The Elementary Forms of the Religious Life* (New York: The Free Press, 1948).

8. Karl Marx, *Capital,* ed. Friedrich Engels (New York: International, 1967).
9. Richard C. Wallace and Wendy D. Wallace, *Sociology,* 2nd ed. (Boston: Allyn and Bacon, 1989), pp. 15, 373.
10. *The Oxford Dictionary of Quotations* (London: Oxford University Press, 1966), p. 240.
11. Richard L. Evans, *Richard Evans' Quote Book* (Salt Lake City, Utah: Publishers Press, 1971), p. 249.
12. Duncan Williams, *Trousered Apes* (Arlington House, 1971), pp. 14-15.
13. John Leo, "Boxing in Believers," *U.S. News & World Report,* September 20, 1993, p. 20.
14. Robert H. Bork, *Slouching Towards Gomorrah: Modern Liberalism and American Decline* (New York: HarperCollins Publishers, Inc., 1996). p. 279.
15. "Secular Rationalism Has Been Unable to Produce a Compelling, Self-justifying Moral Code," *The Chronicle of Higher Education,* April 22, 1992, p. B5.
16. Roger Hendrix, a Speech Delivered to the Annual Luncheon Meeting of the Lawyers Club of Los Angeles County on the Delicate Relationship between Religion and Law, December 16, 1981.
17. Gabriel Almond, Marvin Chodorov, and Ray H. Pearce, "Progress and Its Discontents," *Bulletin of the American Academy of Arts and Sciences,* Vol. 35, 1981, pp. 12-13.
18. Carri P. Jenkins, "The Rise and Demise of Religion," *BYU Today,* June, 1986, p. 40.
19. Bork, *op. cit.,* p. 9.

Chapter 6: The Individual: The Basic Element of Society

1. Jon M. Shepard, *Sociology,* 5th ed. (St. Paul, Minnesota: West Publishing Company, 1993), pp. 137-139.
2. Sterling W. Sill, *The Wealth of Wisdom* (Salt Lake City, Utah: Deseret Book Company, 1977), p. 48.
3. *Descartes Philosophical Writings,* Selected and Translated by Norman K. Smith (New York: Random House, Inc., 1958).
4. Melvin Morse and Paul Perry, *Closer to the Light* (New Jersey: Villard Books, 1990), p. 99.
5. *Ibid.,* pp. 100-101.
6. Melvin Morse and Paul Perry, *Transformed by the Light* (New Jersey: Villard Books, 1992), pp. 195-196.
7. *Ibid.,* pp. 182-183.
8. Robert J. Trotter, "Baby Face," *Psychology Today,* August, 1993, pp. 15-20.

9. Judith Langlois, Lori A. Roggman, Rita J. Casey, Jean M. Ritter, Loretta A. Rieser-Danner, and Vivian Y. Jenkins, "Infant Preferences for Attractive Faces: Rudiments of a Stereotype?," *Developmental Psychology,* 1987, pp. 363-369.
10. Rebecca A. Eder, an Address to the Meeting of the Society for Research in Child Development in Baltimore, Maryland, April 1987.
11. "Social Studies: Babies can be Buddies," *El Paso Times,* March 4, 1991, p. 5C.
12. Craig R. Lundahl and Harold A. Widdison, *The Eternal Journey: How Near-Death Experiences Illuminate Our Earthly Lives* (New York: Warner Books, 1997).
13. "'Your Mother Did It to You' Is An Excuse Americans Overuse," *U.S News and World Report,* March 25, 1985, pp. 63-64.
14. Karen J. Winkler, "Criminals Are Born as Well As Made, Authors of Controversial Book Assert," *The Chronicle of Higher Education,* January 15, 1986, pp. 5, 8.
Flora Johnson, "With Malice Aforethought," *TWA Ambassador,* August, 1979, pp. 79-86.
15. Henry Vaughan, *Silex Scintillans* (1650; second part, 1655).
16. William Wordsworth, *Poems in Two Volumes* (1807).
17. Benjamin Jowett (Trans.), *Dialogues of Plato* (Chicago: Encyclopedia Britannica, 1952), p. 228.
18. *Ibid.,* p. 230.
19. *Great Books of the Western World,* ed. Robert Maynard Hutchings, Vol. 7 (Chicago: Encyclopedia Britannica, Inc., 1952), p. 124.
20. Gladys I. Wade (Ed.), "The Salutation," *The Poetical Works of Thomas Traherne* (London: P. J. and A. E. Dobell, 1932), p. 4.
21. Benjamin Disraeli, "The People's Cyber Nation Quotations," *Internet—http://WWW.Cyber-Nation.com* (December 27, 1997).
22. See Joel M. Charon, *Symbolic Interactionism,* 3rd ed. (Englewood Cliffs, New Jersey: Prentice-Hall, 1989), Chapter 7, for a more detailed description of the human mind.
23. Richard L. Evans, *Richard Evans' Quote Book* (Salt Lake City, Utah: Publishers Press, 1971), p. 19.
24. *Ibid.,* p. 190.
25. Sterling W. Sill, *The Laws of Success* (Salt Lake City, Utah: Deseret Book Company, 1975), p. 49.
26. Shepard, *op. cit.,* pp. 140-141.
27. Gerhard Lenski, Patrick Nolan, and Jean Lenski, *Human Societies: An Introduction to Macrosociology,* 7th ed. (New York: McGraw-Hill, Inc., 1995), p. 441.
28. *Ibid.*
29. Howard W. Hunter, "The Opening and Closing of Doors," *Ensign,* November 1987, p. 59.

30. *Great Books of the Western World,* Vol. 42, p. 256.
31. Duane F. Alwin, Ronald L. Cohen, and Theodore M. Newcomb, *Political Attitudes Over the Life Span: The Bennington Women after Fifty Years* (Madison, Wisconsin: University of Wisconsin Press, 1991).
32. C. A. Hall, *The Home Book of Quotations* (New York: Dodd, Mead & Company, 1935), p. 845.
33. George F. Will, *The Pursuit of Happiness and Other Sobering Thoughts* (New York: Harper/Colophon, 1979).

Chapter 7: Social Relationships: The Connecting Links of Society

1. "Identity Through the Ages," *U.S. News & World Report,* July 1, 1991, p. 59.
2. See Joel M. Charon, *Symbolic Interactionism,* 3rd ed. (Englewood Cliffs, New Jersey: Prentice-Hall 1989), Chapter 3, for a more detailed description of social relationships.

Chapter 8: The Family: The Keystone of Society

1. Hal Williams, "A Tower of Strength Near Failing?" *BYU Today,* December 1980, p. 8.
2. Edward Gibbon, *The Decline and Fall of the Roman Empire,* An Abridgement by D. M. Low, (New York: Harcourt, Brace and Company, 1960).
3. This summary is drawn from John D. Lawrence, *Down to Earth—The Laws of the Harvest* (Portland, Oregon: Multnomah Press, 1975), p. 26.
4. Stuart A. Queen, Robert W. Habenstein, and Jill S. Quadagno, "The Ancient Romans" in *The Family in Various Cultures* (New York: Harper and Row Publishers, Inc., 1985).
5. Karen Kayser Kersten and Lawrence K. Kersten, *Marriage and the Family: Studying Close Relationships* (New York: Harper & Row Publishers, Inc., 1988), pp. 24-25.
   Nicholas S. Timasheff, *The Great Retreat* (New York: E.P. Dutton and Company, Inc., 1946).
6. Carle C. Zimmerman, *Family and Civilization* (New York: Harper and Brothers, 1947).
7. Gerald R. Leslie and Sheila K. Korman, *The Family in Social Context,* 6th ed. (New York: Oxford University Press, 1985), pp. 61-63.

8. Bruce C. Hafen, an Address Delivered to the Fourth Annual Monsignor McDougall Lecture given May 7, 1991 in Salt Lake City under the sponsorship of the Catholic Cathedral of the Madeleine, May 7, 1991.
9. *Ibid.*
10. Arnold Green, *The Nature of Morality* (New York: University Press of America, 1994), p. 88.
11. *Great Treasury of Western Thought,* eds. Mortimer J. Adler and Charles Van Doren (New York: R. R. Bowker Company, 1977), p. 534.
12. Theodore Roosevelt, an Address to the First International Congress in America on the Welfare of the Child, March 1908.
13. A Quote Taken from a Subscription Mailer for *The Family in America* of the Rockford Institute Center on the Famiy in America, 934 N. Main Street, Rockford, Illinois.

Chapter 9: Society: The Sum of Its Membership

1. Richard C. Wallace and Wendy D. Wallace, *Sociology,* 2nd ed. (Boston: Allyn and Bacon, 1989), p. 15.
    Richard E. Johnson, "Inequality: The Haves and the Have-nots," *BYU Today,* September 1990, pp. 47-58.
2. Harold R. Kerbo, *Social Stratification and Inequality: Class Conflict in Historical and Comparative Perspective,* 2nd ed. (New York: McGraw-Hill, Inc., 1991), pp. 134-141.
3. Allan Bloom, *The Closing of the American Mind: How Higher Education has Failed Democracy and Impoverished the Soul of Today's Students* (New York: Simon and Schuster, 1987).
4. David Popenoe, *Sociology,* 4th ed. (Englewood Cliffs, New Jersey: Prentice-Hall, Inc., 1980), pp. 279-284.
5. Kerbo, *op. cit.,* pp. 83, 149-153.
6. Dennis Gilbert and Joseph A. Kahl, *The American Class Structure: A New Synthesis,* 4th ed. (Belmont, California: Wadsworth Publishing Company, 1993), pp. 52-60.
7. Denny Braun, *The Rich Get Richer: The Rise of Income Inequality in the United States and the World* (Chicago: Nelson Hall, Inc., 1991), p. 5.
8. Will Durant and Ariel Durant, *The Lessons of History* (New York: Simon and Schuster, 1968), p. 88.
9. R.P. Cuzzort and E.W. King, *Humanity and Modern Social Thought,* 2nd ed. (Hinsdale, Illinois: Dryden Press, 1976), pp. 131-132.
10. Robert Nisbet, *The Present Age* (New York: Harper & Row, 1988), p. 134.

11. Robert Nisbet, *History of the Idea of Progress* (New York: Basic Books, 1980).
12. Alvin P. Sanoff, "Tradition's Champion," *U.S. News & World Report,* February 18, 1991, pp. 58-59.
13. Durant and Durant, *op. cit.,* p. 75.
14. "Cycling Through U.S. History," *U.S. News & World Report,* December 1, 1986.
15. William Strauss and Neil Howe, *The Fourth Turning* (New York: Broadway Books, 1997).
16. Cheryl Russell, "What Your Birth Order Says About You," *USA Weekend,* May 9-11, 1997, p. 16.
17. *Great Books of the Western World,* ed. Robert Maynard Hutchings, Vol. 32 (Chicago: Encyclopedia Britannica, Inc., 1952), p. 345.
18. Lady Margaret Thatcher, "The Moral Challenges for the Next Century," *Brigham Young Magazine,* August 1996, p. 19.
19. John D. Lawrence, *Down to Earth—The Laws of the Harvest* (Portland, Oregon: Multinomah Press, 1975), p. 27.
20. Karl Marx, *Capital,* ed. Friedrich Engels (New York: International, 1967).
21. *Abraham Lincoln: A Documentary Portrait Through His Speeches and Writings,* ed. Don E. Fehrenbacher (New York: The New American Library, 1964), p. 41.
22. Robert H. Bork, *Slouching Towards Gomorrah: Modern Liberalism and American Decline* (New York: HarperCollins Publishers, Inc., 1996). p. 9.

Chapter 10: The Good Society

1. Robert N. Bellah, Richard Madsen, William M. Sullivan, Ann Swidler, and Steven M. Tipton, *The Good Society* (New York: Alfred M. Knoft, 1992), p. 9.
2. John H. Rhoards, *Critical Issues in Social Theory* (University Park, Pennsylvania: The Pennsylvania State University Press, 1991), pp. 201-202.
3. Steve Brouwer, *Sharing the Pie* (Carlisle, Pennsylvania: Big Picture Books, 1988), p. 1.
4. Adam Smith, *The Theory of Moral Sentiments,* eds. D.D. Raphael and A.L. Macfie (1759; reprint, Oxford: Clarendon Press, 1976), p. 85.
5. Lady Margaret Thatcher, "The Moral Challenges for the Next Century," *Brigham Young Magazine,* August 1996, p. 22.
6. Samuel Bowles, David Gordon, and Thomas Wisskopf, *After the Waste Land: A Democratic Economics for the Year 2000* (Armonk, New York: M.E. Sharpe, Inc., 1990).
7. Brouwer, *op. cit.,* p. 19.

8. Carri P. Jenkins, "Downsizing or Dumbsizing," *Brigham Young Magazine,* Spring 1997, p. 31.
9. *Ibid.*
10. Gerhard Lenski, Patrick Nolan, and Jean Lenski, *Human Societies: An Introduction to Macrosociology,* 7th ed. (New York: McGraw-Hill, Inc., 1995), p. 407.
11. James W. Lucas and Warner P. Woodworth, *Working Toward Zion* (Salt Lake City, Utah: Aspen Books, 1996), p. 312.
12. For other examples of the successful implementation of enterprises utilizing the principles of a cooperative economic system see James W. Lucas and Warner P. Woodworth, *Working Toward Zion* (Salt Lake City, Utah: Aspen Books, 1996).
13. "What Lies Ahead for America?" *Opposing Viewpoints Pamphlets,* ed. David L. Bender (San Diego, California: Greenhaven Press, Inc., 1990), p. 254.
14. Brouwer, *op. cit.,* p. 77.
15. Denny Braun, *The Rich Get Richer: The Rise of Income Inequality in the United States and the World* (Chicago: Nelson Hall, Inc., 1991), p. 284.

Chapter 11: The Restoration of America

1. Francis Fukuyama, *Trust: The Social Virtues and the Creation of Prosperity* (New York: Free Press, 1995).
2. John Leo, "When Stability was all the Rage," *U.S. News & World Report,* October 30, 1995, p. 27.
3. John Leo, "At a Cultural Crossroads," *U.S. News & World Report,* December 20, 1993, p. 14.
4. Gerald Parshall, "Genes, Race and Intelligence," *U.S. News & World Report,* December 27, 1993/January 3, 1994, p. 89.
5. Wray Herbert, "Our Identity Crisis," *U.S. News & World Report,* March 6, 1995, p. 83.
6. *Ibid.*
7. James Fallows, "A Talent for Disorder," *U.S. News & World Report,* February 8, 1988, pp. 83-84.
8. Paul Kennedy, *The Rise and Fall of the Great Powers: Economic Change and Military Conflict from 1500 to 2000* (New York: Random House, 1987).
9. Robert Wuthnow, *Poor Richard's Principle: Recovering the American Dream through the Moral Dimension of Work, Business, and Money* (Princeton, New Jersey: Princeton University Press, 1996).
10. Haynes Johnson, *Divided We Fall: Gambling with History in the Nineties* (New York: W.W. Norton & Company, 1994).

11. *Rebuilding the Nest: A New Commitment to the American Family,* eds. David Blankenhorn, Steven Bayme, and Jean Bethke Elshtain (Milwaukee, Wisconsin: Family Service America, 1990), p. 229.

12. "Is America in Decline?" *Opposing Viewpoints Pamphlets,* ed. David L. Bender (San Diego, California: Greenhaven Press, Inc., 1990), p. 111.

    Robert H. Bork, *Slouching Towards Gomorrah: Modern Liberalism and American Decline* (New York: HarperCollins Publishers, Inc., 1996). p. 277.

    "America Sees a Spiritual Awakening," *U.S. News & World Report,* December 25, 1995/January 1, 1996, p. 85.

13. Lady Margaret Thatcher, "The Moral Challenges for the Next Century," *Brigham Young Magazine,* August 1996, p. 18.

14. Ezra Taft Benson, *This Nation Shall Endure* (Salt Lake City, Utah: Deseret Book Company, 1977), p. 28.

15. *Ibid.,* p. 16.

16. Ezra Taft Benson, *The Constitution: A Heavenly Banner* (Salt Lake City, Utah: Deseret Book Company, 1986), p. 11.

17. David Barton, *America: To Pray or Not to Pray* (Aledo, Texas: Wallbuilder Press, 1988) pp. viii-ix.

18. *Ibid.,* p. xii.

19. *Ibid.*

20. "How do Religious Values Influence America?" *Opposing Viewpoints Pamphlets,* ed. David L. Bender (San Diego, California: Greenhaven Press, Inc., 1990), p. 214.

21. Barton, *op. cit.*

22. Gordon B. Hinckley, an Address Delivered to America's Freedom Festival in Provo, Utah, June 26, 1988.

23. Joseph Addison (pseudonym for Angus McDonald), *The St. Croix Review,* Vol. 1, No. 1 (1967), pp. 6-7.

24. *Great Treasury of Western Thought,* eds. Mortimer J. Adler and Charles Van Doren (New York: R. R. Bowker Company, 1977), p. 1083.

25. Edith Hamilton, *The Roman Way* (New York: Avon Books, 1960).

26. Richard C. Wallace and Wendy D. Wallace, *Sociology,* 2nd ed. (Boston: Allyn and Bacon, 1989), p. 373.

27. Barton, *op. cit.,* p. xii.

28. Wallace and Wallace, *loc. cit.*

29. Kennedy, *The Rise and Fall of the Great Powers: Economic Change and Military Conflict from 1500 to 2000.*

30. Wallace and Wallace, *op. cit.,* p. 65.

31. Denny Braun, *The Rich Get Richer: The Rise of Income Inequality in the United States and the World* (Chicago: Nelson Hall, Inc., 1991), p. 20.

1991), p. 20.

32. David Crowder, "What's Missing from Schools? Maybe Principles Found in History," *El Paso Times,* n.d.

Chapter 12: Some Thoughts on Global Society

1. Keith McFarland, a Speech to the National Convention of the Independent Petroleum Association of America, 1976.

2. C.S. Lewis, *Mere Christianity* (New York: MacMillan Co., 1958), p. 39.

3. Will Durant and Ariel Durant, *The Story of Civilization,* Vol. 3 (New York: Simon and Schuster, 1944), p. 665.

4. Hugh W. Nibley, *Since Cumorah* (Salt Lake City, Utah: Deseret Book Company, 1967), p. 425.

5. "Is America in Decline?" *Opposing Viewpoints Pamphlets,* ed. David L. Bender (San Diego, California: Greenhaven Press, Inc., 1995), p. 112.

6. "Global Gap Widens Between Rich, Poor," *El Paso Times,* July 16, 1996.

7. Daniel E. Rossides, *Social Stratification: The American Class System in Comparative Perspective* (Englewood Cliffs, New Jersey: Prentice Hall, 1990), p. 519.

8. Chief Seattle, Testimony, in 1854.

9. Harrison Rainie with Margaret Loftus and Mark Madden, "The State of Greed," *U.S. News & World Report,* June 17, 1996, pp. 68.

Index

Author Biography

Craig R. Lundahl, Ph.D., has had the opportunity to serve in a variety of capacities throughout his career including those of sociologist, demographer, author, educator, administrator, social researcher, social scientist, grantsman, and consultant.

Presently, he is Professor Emeritus of Sociology and Business Administration and Chair Emeritus of the Department of Social Sciences at Western New Mexico University in Silver City, New Mexico and serves as Senior Professor at Senior University in Richmond, British Columbia, Canada.

Dr. Lundahl received a Bachelor of Science Degree in sociology from Brigham Young University, and Master of Science and Doctor of Philosophy Degrees in sociology from Utah State University. He has done postdoctoral work at Harvard University and the University of Michigan.

He is the author of a number of articles and books and has presented his work nationally and internationally. He was a pioneer researcher on solar energy technology diffusion, planning and evaluation in higher education, and the near-death experience. He received international recognition as the organizer and leader of the world's leading research teams on solar energy technology diffusion in the mid-1970s when he presented research in London, England and on rational planning and evaluation in higher education in the early 1980s when he presented research along with his colleagues from the University of Michigan in Paris, France.

He is also nationally and internationally recognized for his work in near-death studies and has presented his work nationally in New York

City, San Antonio, Salt Lake City, and St. Louis and internationally in Canada and Italy. He has studied near-death experiences since 1977.

His lifetime's work as a scholar has concentrated on understanding and explaining the total spectrum of social life and part of his findings have been published by Warner Books in the 1997 book, *The Eternal Journey: How Near-Death Experiences Illuminate Our Earthly Lives* (coauthored with Harold A. Widdison), and his other findings are contained in this volume, *The Nature of Humanity and the State of America: A Unified Theory of the Social World.* He has completed another book entitled, *The End of Time and The Millennium of Peace: NDE Prophetic Visions and Holy Prophecies on Life Before and During the Next Millennium,* which depicts the future of society into the twenty-first century and social life in the new society of the next millennium.

The Test of Truth is Time